The Ghost in the Addict

The Ghost in the Addict

Shepard Siegel

The MIT Press
Cambridge, Massachusetts
London, England

© 2024 Massachusetts Institute of Technology

All rights reserved. No part of this book may be used to train artificial intelligence systems or reproduced in any form by any electronic or mechanical means (including photocopying, recording, or information storage and retrieval) without permission in writing from the publisher.

The MIT Press would like to thank the anonymous peer reviewers who provided comments on drafts of this book. The generous work of academic experts is essential for establishing the authority and quality of our publications. We acknowledge with gratitude the contributions of these otherwise uncredited readers.

This book was set in Stone Serif and Stone Sans by Westchester Publishing Services. Printed and bound in the United States of America.

Library of Congress Cataloging-in-Publication Data

Names: Siegel, Shepard, author.
Title: The ghost in the addict / Shepard Siegel.
Description: Cambridge, Massachusetts : The MIT Press, [2024] | Includes bibliographical references and index.
Identifiers: LCCN 2023024013 (print) | LCCN 2023024014 (ebook) | ISBN 9780262547970 (paperback) | ISBN 9780262378505 (epub) | ISBN 9780262378512 (pdf)
Subjects: LCSH: Drug addiction. | Drug addiction—Treatment.
Classification: LCC HV5801 .S467 2024 (print) | LCC HV5801 (ebook) | DDC 362.29—dc23/eng/20231024
LC record available at https://lccn.loc.gov/2023024013
LC ebook record available at https://lccn.loc.gov/2023024014

10 9 8 7 6 5 4 3 2 1

To Laura and Jeffrey and Marcia

Contents

Preface and Acknowledgments ix

1 The Haunting of the Addict 1
2 The Failure of Legislation 5
3 The Heroin Overdose Mystery 11
4 Why Addicts Usually Don't Overdose 25
5 Why Addicts Sometimes Overdose: Opiate Expectancy and Effects 31
6 Ivan P. Pavlov, Walter B. Cannon, and Homeostasis 43
7 Learning and Drug Tolerance 49
8 Alcohol Expectancy and Alcohol's Effect 57
9 Victimized by Pavlovian Conditioning 67
10 The Geographic Cure 81
11 Expected and Unexpected Drugs 95
12 Evocative Effects of a Small Drug Dose 107
13 Images, Cognitions, and Emotions as Cues for Drugs 113
14 Problems with Treating Addiction 117
15 The Special Case of Cigarettes 127
16 Why Doesn't Everyone Become an Addict? 131

17 Does Addiction Result in Brain Damage? 137
18 To Be Addicted 143

Notes 147
Index 175

Preface and Acknowledgments

Over half a century ago I first started my research on the Pavlovian conditioning of drug effects in rats. In 1972 the drug I used was insulin, and the effect of interest was blood-sugar level. Insulin lowers blood sugar—a hypoglycemic response. After a number of daily insulin injections, each following a distinctive drug administration ritual, the rat was injected with an inert substance, physiological saline, following the usual drug-administration ritual. This physiological saline injection produced an elevation in blood-sugar levels—a hyperglycemic response. The anticipation of hypoglycemia induced hyperglycemia.[1] A few years later it occurred to me that an anticipatory response that attenuates the drug effect might be a mechanism of drug tolerance—that is, the decreasing effect of a drug over the course of successive administrations—a hypothesis that I was able to confirm.[2]

What about the situation in which expected tolerance seems insufficient? Often an experienced heroin addict dies from an apparent overdose of the drug. A well-written article about ostensible heroin overdose that I read in the *New York Times* in 1972 made a lasting impression on me. It was written by a science journalist, Edward Brecher, and was titled "So

Why Do Heroin Addicts Drop Dead?"[3] Brecher's insights into heroin overdose were extraordinary. He summarized a mass of data indicating that the so-called overdose victims died following self-administration of a dose of heroin that would not be expected to kill these drug-experienced, and therefore drug-tolerant, individuals. Although the profundity of his contribution was not immediately recognized, 44 years later a well-known addiction researcher, Shane Darke, stated, "in one chapter, Brecher laid the foundations for all subsequent overdose research."[4] Some of that subsequent research was conducted in my laboratory. We hypothesized that tolerance would fail to occur if the anticipatory response responsible for tolerance failed to occur. The anticipatory response would fail to occur if the drug was not taken following the usual drug administration ritual, but rather it was taken in a novel environment not previously paired with the drug. Our hypothesis was confirmed.[5]

The anticipatory drug response is adaptive. It can save the addict's life. In that same year, 1982, we considered circumstances in which the occurrence of the anticipatory drug response was problematic. What if the addict is in the presence of the usual drug-paired cues but there's no drug to administer? That is, the individual is in an environment where he or she has frequently used drugs in the past, or it is the time of day when the drug typically is administered, or any of a variety of drug-paired stimuli are present. In the situation in which the addict has learned to expect the drug but does not receive the drug, drug anticipatory responses would achieve full expression because they are not countered by any drug effect. The learned anticipatory responses exhibited in such circumstances typically are not recognized or labeled as a drug-anticipatory learned responses. Rather, they are (mis-)labeled drug "withdrawal symptoms": "There is, in fact, much evidence suggesting that stimuli normally associated with drug administration elicit so-called withdrawal symptoms . . . Many addicts report that these symptoms are strong motivators for the resumption of drug taking."[6] Most addicts are unaware that the drug anticipatory response is elicited by drug-paired stimuli. Rather, they just experience drug-preparatory responses from time to time. The drug preparation/withdrawal set of symptoms elicited by drug-paired stimuli is the ghost that haunts the addict.

Much of my research in subsequent years, usually with talented collaborators, has elaborated on the role of the drug-anticipatory response in addiction. It is now clear that the anticipatory response is a basic mechanism of adaptation. The drug has profound physiological effects that can actually threaten the survival of the drug-taker. The addict's preparation for the drug in the presence of drug-paired cues minimizes the detrimental effect of the drug. The ghost that haunts the addict can be a compassionate ghost. It potentially saves the addict's life.

There is the widespread view that addiction is evidence of a pathology wherein withdrawal is a symptom. In fact, the addict has a healthy and adaptive response to the bodily changes caused by the drug. He or she has learned to prepare for the drug in anticipation of the physiological upheaval induced by the drug. These preparatory responses (mistakenly considered as drug-withdrawal symptoms) have wrongly been thought to be due to the baneful effects of the previous drug administrations, rather than the preparatory response for the next drug administration.

There is increasing concern that terms such as "addict" and "drug abuser" are stigmatizing. According to the head of the National Institute on Drug Abuse, Nora Volkow, these terms neglect to emphasize that people who continually self-administer drugs are suffering from a disorder. She and her colleagues suggest a more person-centered language, e.g., replacing "addict" with "a person having a substance use disorder."[7] This approach to terminology is problematic. A largely historical analysis of the literature of excessive drug and alcohol use would have to change terms that have been in use for many years. For example, rather than "Alcoholics Anonymous," we'd have "Persons with an Alcohol Abuse Disorder Anonymous"; in addition, many scientific journals maintain the use of "addiction" in their title: *Addiction, Addiction Biology, Addictive Behaviors, Journal of Addictive Medicine, Psychology of Addictive Behaviors, American Journal of Addiction*, and many more. More importantly, use of the new terminology would suggest agreement with the National Institute on Drug Abuse's commitment to a brain disorder view of excessive drug use. It has taken me 50 years to realize that drug addiction is not a "disorder." It is not an indication of a diseased brain, but rather, it is a manifestation of homeostasis. To use the terminology of Walter Cannon, it's an expression of "the wisdom of the body."[8]

The research that has led to that realization was funded primarily by the U.S. National Institute on Drug Abuse and the National Research Council of Canada. This drug-conditioning research has been done in conjunction with the work of many others. For over 30 years the research was facilitated by the diligence and creativity of Doreen Mitchell, my research technician and collaborator. Over the years I have benefited enormously from discussions with my colleague Lorraine Allan. My discussions with Barry Dworkin have done much to clarify my thinking about Pavlovian conditioning in general, and the Pavlovian conditioning of drug responses in particular.

Many graduate students contributed to the drug-conditioning research and have provided insights into the role of learning in drug tolerance: Marco Baptista, Tom Eissenberg, Tina Goodison, Riley Hinson, Joseph Kim, Marvin Krank, Susan Larson, Glenda MacQueen, James MacRae, Robert McDonald, Barbara Ramos, Marta Sokolowska, and Lori Weise-Kelly. Finally, I am indebted to Marcia Frank for her critical reading of various drafts of the book, and for so much more, for the past 35 years.

1 The Haunting of the Addict

> The dead drug leaves a ghost behind. At certain hours it haunts the house.
> —Jean Cocteau, *Opium: The Diary of a Cure*, translated by M. Crosland and S. Road (New York: Grove Press, 1958 [1930]), 60

People who have a drug addiction, clinicians who treat these people, and scientists who study addictive behavior all agree on one thing: the real problem in treating addiction is relapse following treatment. It's not an overwhelming problem to get people to stop using drugs for a time. To paraphrase an observation variously attributed to W. C. Fields, Mark Twain, and others: "It's easy to stop drinking—I've done it a thousand times." However, people who stop drinking or smoking or using other drugs, for weeks and even years, report that withdrawal symptoms and cravings spontaneously reappear. Former addicts are bedeviled by some tenacious remnant of their prior drug experience.

The persistent residue of addiction was described by the poet Barbara Greenberg. Her addiction was to nicotine, not opium, but she, too, used spectral imagery. Long after her last cigarette, she was (like Jean Cocteau) still pursued by a ghost:

> How long has it been since I smoked? Four years? Five?
> My father died—and then there were changes right and left
> in my life. I moved. I broke with friends. I had my hair cut short,
> and I quit smoking. "That's it, motherweed," I announced; I quit
> cold turkey! Ah, but I am no more rid of it than the faith
> I was born into, or the dear ones from whom I am now
> estranged, or any blue ghost . . . [1]

Barbara Greenberg was haunted by a "blue ghost," the residual effects of her previous smoking history, years after she stopped smoking. Opiate users similarly display withdrawal symptoms long after their last drug administration,[2] as do alcohol users.[3] What summons this ghost? Why does the former drug user, abstinent for days, weeks, months, or years, still experience craving and withdrawal distress from time to time? It seems as if the cravings spontaneously occur. The individual may be doing fine and drug-free for a considerable period of time. Suddenly they are overcome by withdrawal distress—a persistent craving for the drug, and frequently relapse to drug use. As noted by the sociologist Patrick Biernacki, "the tendency of some people to relapse, and become readdicted, often after long periods of abstinence, is a perplexing aspect to addiction and a feature that should be addressed in any theory attempting to explain it."[4]

In fact, perceptive observers realized for a long time that the ghost's appearance was not arbitrary. Rather, the ghost appears when the individual that has used drugs is in the presence of stimuli that have been associated with the drug—places, times, thoughts, and circumstances that, in the past, had been paired with drug use. These drug-paired stimuli might be internal as well as external. For example, stress, anxiety, or depression may have been experienced prior to each drug use. When these external or internal stimuli are present, the risk of relapse is especially pronounced. The individual may not be aware that the ghost appears when drug-paired stimuli occur. He or she may simply experience withdrawal distress from time to time but not recognize the relationship between drug-paired stimuli and the reappearance of motivation to use the drug. Nevertheless, the importance of drug-associated situations in relapse was known to some of those concerned about the most common form of drug abuse in colonial America—alcohol.

Many inhabitants of colonial America subscribed to the 1673 opinion of the Puritan clergyman, Increase Mather: "Drink is in itself a creature of God, and to be received with thankfulness."[5] However, concerns did develop about excessive drinking in pre-Revolutionary America, especially after the distilling industry became well established. The first commercial distillery opened in Boston. Boston, New Haven, Philadelphia, and Providence became centers for this very profitable business, and by 1770 there were over 140 distilleries.[6] Many in America developed a taste for the rum (and later grain spirits) that now were widely available and inexpensive. The Continental army was a huge whiskey consumer; a substantial daily liquor ration was provided to American Revolutionary soldiers.

Benjamin Rush was a colonial physician who cautioned about the health problems of excessive alcohol consumption. Rush was the most eminent American physician at the time of the Revolutionary War. He was surgeon general with the Continental Army (until he became critical of George Washington's leadership and resigned). Dr. Rush was a member of the Continental Congress and a signer of the Declaration of Independence. He wrote the first chemistry and psychiatry textbooks in the United States. He actively promoted a variety of social causes, and also was concerned about the problem of alcoholism in the early days of the republic. He noted an important feature of alcoholism—the "operation of the human mind which obliges it to associate ideas, accidentally or otherwise combined."[7] Alcohol is one such idea, and the alcoholic is obliged to associate certain places and times with alcohol. Rush observed that it is in these alcohol-associated situations that withdrawal distress and craving for drink is pronounced, and avoiding these situations facilitates abstinence:

> Some men drink only in the morning, some at noon, and some at night. Some men drink only on a market day, some at one tavern only, and some only in one kind of company. Now by finding a new and interesting employment, or subject of conversation for drunkards at the usual times in when they have been accustomed to drink, and by restraining them by the same means from those places and companions, which suggested to them the idea of ardent spirits, their habits of intemperance may be completely destroyed.[8]

The more we learn about addiction, the more we realize the profundity of Dr. Rush's observations. The importance of context in drug use—the time, the place, the company present at the time of use—is the key to understanding addiction. The idea that relapse is often seen in the presence of stimuli that have been paired with drug use has constantly been rediscovered by successive generations of researchers, and repeatedly presented as a new and innovative insight into the addictive mind. It was not until a century after Rush died that tools for the study of associations between paired events were developed, and another century passed before the importance of our obligation "to associate ideas" (including the idea of a drug) with prevailing context was well established.

By understanding the role of drug-paired cues in addiction we can understand why people become addicted and why treatment is difficult, and determine ways we can focus our energy and resources in dealing with drug use. This understanding, unfortunately, was lacking by the policymakers who promoted anti-drug legislation in the early years of the twentieth century.

2 The Failure of Legislation

> It is well-established that the ordinary case of addiction yields to proper treatment, and that addicts will remain permanently cured when drug taking is stopped and they are otherwise physically restored to health and strengthened in will power.
> —United States Treasury Department, 1921. Reprinted in Charles E. Terry and Mildred Pellins, *The Opium Problem* (Montclair, NJ: Patterson Smith, 1970 [1928]), 758

From the time of the founding of the United States until the early part of the twentieth century there was very little in the way of restrictive legislation concerning drug use. All manner of addictive substances, and paraphernalia for administering them, were widely available in drug stores and general stores. Various preparations of opium, such as laudanum (opium dissolved in alcohol) and paregoric (powdered opium mixed with a variety of inactive ingredients), as well as cocaine-containing beverages and hypodermic syringes, were in the Sears-Roebuck catalog as recently as 1897. In many places in the United States (and Great Britain) per-capita consumption of highly addictive drugs, like opium, was far in excess of any current levels: "The high Victorians, in fact, were often high."[1]

Although some expressed alarm about the pernicious effects of drugs, the users generally were simply considered to be people with annoying and unwholesome habits. Those that had concerns about excessive drug use did not focus on opium, but rather on alcohol. In fact, there were many clinicians who recommended turning people who were intractable alcoholics into people who were addicted to morphine. As Dr. J. R. Black stated in 1889, "as a whole, the use of morphine in place of alcohol is but a choice of evils, and by far the lesser."[2] There were temperance movements that advocated control of alcohol availability, and even prohibition, but they were generally seen as extremist organizations. There were few attempts to prohibit the use of drugs.

The way we thought about drugs and drug-users changed dramatically in the early decades of the twentieth century. Politicians in the United States were seized by a prohibitionist frenzy. In 1917 Congress submitted the Eighteenth Amendment to the Constitution to states for ratification. The necessary three-quarters majority was reached a little over one year later, and alcohol prohibition went into effect in 1920. By 1922, fifteen states had prohibited the sale of cigarettes, and some others had imposed such onerous taxes that cigarettes were essentially not legally available.[3] These acts subsequently were repealed. However, one act passed in this whirlwind of anti-drug sentiment has only been strengthened over the years—the Harrison Narcotics Act (officially titled, "An Act to provide for the registration of, with collectors of internal revenue, and to impose a special tax upon all persons who produce, import, manufacture, compound, deal in, dispense sell distribute, or give away opium or coca leaves, their salts, derivatives, or preparations, and for other purposes").[4] The Harrison Narcotics Act, named after its sponsor, New York

The Failure of Legislation

congressman Francis Burton Harrison, was passed in 1914, implemented in 1915, and strengthened as a result of subsequent legislation and judicial decisions. What had been lawful activity for perhaps a quarter of a million drug users was made illegal. These legislators did not realize that they were dealing with remarkably tenacious behavior. They thought that most addicts would simply obey the law and give up their habits. There was a general consensus that although some drug users might have moderately uncomfortable withdrawal symptoms when the newly prohibited drugs became unavailable, the discomfort would pass in about a week, and the former addicts would be as good as new. There was no recognition of the ghost that would continue to haunt the addict. In the early years of the Harrison Act enforcement attempts were made to provide long-term addicts with maintenance-levels of drug, but subsequent interpretations of the act made it clear that abstinence was required.

It soon became apparent that the cessation of drug use was not something that could be imposed simply by legislative fiat. Indeed, once the withdrawal period had passed, the treated addict often did seem to be cured and looked forward to a new, drug-free life. It soon became apparent that this optimism was short-lived. Merely waiting out the withdrawal symptoms was not sufficient to overcome addiction. Enforced abstinence, in a treatment facility or in prison, was, in the vast majority of cases, followed by relapse to drug use following release. Even after very protracted periods of abstinence, "detoxified" addicts would, with few exceptions, return to drug use. The ghost reasserted itself.

The reasons for post-treatment relapse intrigued Lawrence Kolb, an Assistant Surgeon General of the United States Public Health Service. In the 1920s he noted that apparently successfully treated addicts again experienced drug withdrawal symptoms and craving when confronted with situations that had been paired with drug use. Kolb illustrated the phenomenon with the example of tobacco: "We see this plainly exemplified in the cured tobacco smoker . . . A cured smoker who usually does not crave tobacco may feel an intense desire resembling hunger when he gazes on a box of cigars or sits in the company of friends who are smoking."[5] Kolb noted a similar phenomenon in opiate addicts: "Nearly all of those who have abstained from narcotics for several months report that they have no desire for the drugs unless they see someone else take them or unless they associate with other addicts in situations which they formerly enjoyed."[6] Kolb noted that even after treatment addicts would relapse when they returned to their old environment. For example, he stated:

> A large proportion of the psychopaths, who with full knowledge of its danger, had dissipated with an opiate until they became addicts, were unable to give any reason for their relapses that occurred during the first three years of their addiction. Many of them frankly said that they just started to take the drug again and had no excuse to offer other than that they returned to their old environment.[7]

Kolb rediscovered a phenomenon described by Benjamin Rush over 120 years previously.

In the 1920s prisons were filling up with the newly criminalized narcotics addicts. The penal system was overwhelmed. To deal with the influx of addict-prisoners, a seemingly compassionate solution was reached. The "Narcotic Farm" was established in Lexington, Kentucky, and opened in 1935. Under the joint supervision of the Bureau of Prisons and the Public Health Service, the 1,000-acre facility was devoted to treating addicts for their addiction. Lawrence Kolb was the first superintendent of the Narcotic Farm. He stated that the farm marked

The Failure of Legislation

a new era in the control of addiction: "Now addicts will no longer be merely sent to prison for what is really a weakness, but will be given the best medical treatment that science can afford in an atmosphere designed to rehabilitate them spiritually, mentally, and physically."[8] The "best medical treatment" consisted of vocational therapy and psychotherapy. The "cure" failed, and by 1969 the farm instituted a new treatment strategy. Rather than vocational therapy, addicts were subjected to unremitting peer pressure to give up their drug use. This strategy also failed, with the relapse rate for Narcotic Farm alumni holding steady at about 90 percent. In 1979 the Narcotic Farm was finally declared a failure and closed.[9]

Again and again, contemporary drug researchers have discovered the powerful influence of the ghost conjured by drug-associated stimuli. Such residual effects of prior drug use, even in long-abstinent former drug users, provide us with a profound understanding of addiction. There is a general view that addiction is "maladaptive." It seems like a pattern of behavior that is contrary to our evolutionary heritage of rational, life-preserving actions—"the wisdom of the body." Addiction is perplexing because it seems like a case of "a seeming unwisdom of the body."[10] In fact, the ghost that haunts the addict is, as we shall see, evidence of the addict's adaptive response to pharmacological threat. Although the apparition may create mischief, it also protects the addict from mortal danger. We will consider the case of heroin overdose next.

3 The Heroin Overdose Mystery

> Continued utilization of the term "overdose" to cover all heroin-related fatalities may be counterproductive in developing strategies to reduce the morbidity and mortality associated with heroin.
> —Shane Darke and Deborah Zador, "Fatal Heroin 'Overdose':
> A Review," *Addiction* (December 1996): 1770

Being a heroin addict is not easy. In addition to negotiating the many pitfalls of participation in a criminal subculture, the addict faces the ever-present threat of death by overdose. Heroin, like other opiate drugs, suppresses activity in the part of the brain that controls breathing. Sometimes the drug has such a pronounced depressive effect on respiration that the drug-taker stops breathing and dies. Although substantial tolerance develops to the respiratory depressive effects of heroin (that is, the drug-experienced individual can survive a dose many times greater than that which would kill the drug-inexperienced individual), it appears that this tolerance often is insufficient. Each year, 1 to 3 percent of heroin users die from overdose.[1] The illicitly supplied heroin is of unknown purity, and many addicts pursue ever-higher highs. It would seem that sometimes addicts simply take too much of the drug—enough to overcome their tolerance.

Such a view of heroin overdose has come under increasing scrutiny. Surprisingly, the major impetus for re-evaluation of the mechanisms for heroin overdose came not from scientists, but rather from a science journalist, Edward Brecher. In the era of drug hysteria surrounding President Nixon's 1971 call for a "war on drugs," Brecher authored (under the aegis of *Consumer Reports* magazine) a sober and dispassionate analysis of drug use, *Licit and Illicit Drugs*. In that book he made the compelling case that "(1) the deaths cannot be due to overdose. (2) there never has been any evidence that they are due to overdose. (3) there has long been a plethora of evidence that they are not due to overdose"; "These deaths are, if anything, associated with 'underdose' rather than overdose," he wrote.[2] It is difficult to overestimate Brecher's contribution to understanding overdose. According to the noted addiction researcher, Shane Darke, "in one chapter, Brecher laid the foundations for all subsequent overdose research."[3] Brecher presented the evidence for these assertions in a chapter with the same title as this chapter. The bit of plagiarism is an homage to him.

Brecher summarized evidence concerning the misapplication of the term "overdose" that was available in 1972, when *Licit and Illicit Drugs* was published. The points he made are still valid. For example, a case report of a heroin overdose written 33 years after the publication of *Licit and Illicit Drugs* illustrates many of the enigmatic features of such "overdoses" that Brecher discussed. In 2005, a Hungarian research group, headed by József Gerevich, described the curious events surrounding the death of a heroin addict (identified as "K. J.") in Budapest on January 29, 1999.[4] The events were reconstructed from the medical report, and from information given by drug-using friends who were with the addict on the day that he died. K. J., along with these friends, bought heroin from a dealer. Later that day K. J. was found dead. A syringe containing heroin solution, and a spoon of the sort used for cooking the diluted heroin mixture prior to injection, were beside the body. Metabolites of heroin were found in K. J.'s blood and urine. Not surprisingly, the authorities concluded that K. J. suffered a heroin overdose.

There were, however, several puzzling features of this apparent heroin overdose. Despite that fact that a number of people (in addition to K. J.) bought heroin from the same dealer at the same time, only K. J. died. The other purchasers reported that they had no problems with the drug. Moreover, postmortem examination revealed that the concentration of morphine in K. J.'s blood (heroin is metabolized to morphine) was a fraction of that required to kill an experienced heroin addict who had presumably developed substantial tolerance to the drug. In fact, the amount of drug that K. J. administered on January 29 (the day he died) was about the same that he administered on January 28, with no toxic reaction occurring on the day before his death. Moreover, the postmortem examination provided no evidence that K. J. had administered other drugs (alcohol, barbiturates, benzodiazepines) in conjunction with heroin.

As noted by the authors of this case report, these observations of the puzzling circumstances of K. J.'s death are not unprecedented. It has been known for some time that addicts who die shortly after administering heroin typically have blood-morphine levels that are not higher than those seen in addicts who do not suffer an overdose, or who die from other drug-unrelated causes after self-administering heroin.[5] For example, in 1977 Joseph Monforte, a toxicologist in the Wayne County (Detroit area) Medical Examiner's Office, reported that about three quarters of heroin overdose victims had blood levels of morphine no higher than those seen in a control group of heroin addicts who died as a result of homicide (rather than heroin overdose). In summarizing his findings, Monforte stated, "one must conclude that in the great majority of [overdose] cases death was not the result of a toxic quantity of morphine in the blood."[6]

A decade prior to Monforte's report, Milton Helpern, the Chief Medical Examiner of New York City, concluded, "there does not appear to be a quantitative correlation between the acute fulminating lethal effect and the amount of heroin taken."[7] Consistent with the 2005 report of K. J.'s death, in 1967 Helpern and others noted that a fatal reaction to heroin may occur despite the fact that the individual self-administered a comparable dose the prior day with no ill effects, and that it is common for a number of users to take drugs from the same batch, but only rarely does more than one suffer a life-threatening reaction.[8] A more recent study compared blood-morphine levels in overdose victims with those of automobile drivers who were arrested for suspicion of opiate intoxication (but did not suffer an overdose).[9] There was considerable overlap in the blood morphine levels of the two populations. As noted in a recent summary of this literature the addiction researcher, Shane Darke, concluded: "blood morphine concentrations in fatal cases are frequently below those of intoxicated heroin users, or users who died due to causes other than drug toxicity."[10]

It would seem that K. J.'s death, and the deaths of many other heroin addicts, are not true overdoses, as the term is usually understood. Rather, the addicts die from "underdoses." As indicated in a study of heroin overdose victims in the District of Columbia, "the term 'overdose' has served to indicate lack of understanding of the true mechanism of deaths in fatalities directly related to opiate use."[11] Despite the likely misuse of the word, it is convenient to use the generally accepted term "heroin overdose" when referring to these perplexing fatalities, rather than more cumbersome alternatives such as that offered by the addiction researcher, Charles Cherubin—"an idiosyncratic reaction to an intravenous injection of unspecific material(s) and probably not a true pharmacologic overdose of narcotics."[12] The basis for this "idiosyncratic reaction" has been a mystery. In the words of Temple University psychiatrist Arnold Werner, "it remains unclear why a given dose of heroin will cause this reaction at one time and not at others."[13]

Various hypotheses have been advanced to explain these deaths. Heroin is often bulked up with various contaminants, such as quinine, caffeine, or sucrose. The addict does not know the content of the illicitly obtained drug, and some have suggested that such contaminants are responsible for apparent heroin overdoses. There is little evidence to support such role for contaminants. After an exhaustive examination of the heroin overdose literature, Shane Darke concluded, "if we have learnt one thing over the past 25 years, it is that contaminants play little, if any, role in opioid overdose."[14]

Heroin addicts are frequently polydrug users, often taking other central nervous system depressants, such as alcohol and benzodiazepines, and the fatal reaction may be attributable to an exaggeration of the effect of heroin by these other drugs that are concomitantly used. Indeed, some cases of heroin overdose may be attributable to the interaction of heroin with other drugs;[15] however, there are many cases that (like K. J.) involve heroin overdose death in the absence of the other drugs.

Others have suggested that the addict may overdose if he or she has recently been abstinent (either self-initiated abstinence, or abstinence as result of incarceration). According to this interpretation, the tolerance that had built up during a prolonged period of drug use, and that would be expected to protect the addict from the lethal effect of the drug, will have dissipated during the prolonged, drug-free period.[16] This interpretation would not be relevant to K. J.'s overdose, as he was not abstinent prior to his final drug injection. Moreover, there is evidence that tolerance typically does not substantially dissipate merely with the passage of time. There is considerable retention of tolerance, over a protracted drug-free period of many months,[17] or even years,[18] in human addicts. Similar findings have been reported in experiments with rats.[19]

Further evidence that abstinence-induced loss of tolerance cannot explain overdose comes from objective examination of the overdose victim's premorbid drug use history. A record of an addict's drug use is written in his or her hair. It is possible to reconstruct this record, including periods of abstinence, using a technique called "segmental hair analysis." Many drugs, and drug metabolites, diffuse from the blood stream into the growing hair shaft. The evidence of the drug remains in place as the hair grows. Although hair from any part of the body may be evaluated, scalp hair is especially informative. This hair grows about 1 centimeter per month. Drug-positive bands in this hair can be evaluated, and drug free segments indicate periods of no drug use. Extensive hair growth between periods of opiate detection would mean that the individual had been abstinent for some period of time. Such an analysis of hair of recently deceased addicts in Stockholm was undertaken to see if there was evidence for the abstinence hypothesis. There wasn't, and the authors concluded that "abstinence is not a critical factor for heroin overdose death."[20]

So why did K. J. die? Although Edward Brecher indicated that so-called overdoses were a mystery, he did not know, in 1972, about a more recently discovered solution to the mystery—the novelty of the drug-administration environment. Addicts who administer the drug in a place other that their usual drug-administration environment are at risk for overdose. Gerevich and colleagues noted that a distinctive aspect of K. J.'s final drug administration was the location of the event—a public toilet. Although this is not an unusual place to inject heroin for many addicts, it was a novel administration environment for K. J. K. J., who had used heroin for about four years, had not previously injected himself in a toilet. Rather, he and his wife (also a heroin addict) habitually shot up together at home, and they did so on January 28—the day before the overdose. However, on January 29, he departed from his usual routine of returning home with his heroin purchase and sharing the drug with his wife. Rather, earlier that day K. J. and his wife promised each other that they would begin a period of drug abstinence—a promise that K. J. quickly broke. So as not to confront his wife with his continued drug use, K. J. clandestinely self-administered the drug, by himself rather than in the company of his wife, and in a place where he had not previously injected himself. There was nothing unusual about the drug or the dose that K. J. administered on January 29. What was unusual was the novelty of the setting. However, attributing K. J.'s death to the unusual (for him) physical location of the fatal injection might seem unlikely. How can the drug-administration environment potentiate the effect of a drug? Gerevich and colleagues pointed out, however, that there were precedents for this observation.

Consider a report of the curious features of an apparent overdose death of a patient receiving morphine for relief of pain caused by advanced pancreatic cancer.[21] The patient (identified as "N. E.") was receiving palliative care at his home in Pennsylvania and received a morphine injection four times per day. Either one of the patient's two sons injected the opiate in accordance with procedures specified by the patient's physician. Typically, the preparation of the injection was observed by both sons to assure accuracy. The injections had been given for four weeks. N. E.'s condition was such that he stayed in his bedroom, which was dimly lit and contained the hospital-type apparatus necessary for his care. The morphine had always been injected while N. E. was in this environment. For some reason, on the day that the overdose occurred, N. E. dragged himself out of the bedroom to the living room. The living room was brightly lit and different in many ways from the bedroom/sickroom. N. E., discovered in the living room by one of his sons, appeared to be in considerable pain. Inasmuch as it was time for his father's scheduled morphine injection, the son injected the drug while his father was in the living room. N. E. had never previously received morphine in this environment. Even though there was no evidence that there was anything unusual about the dose of morphine administered on this occasion, N. E. suffered an opiate overdose and died. The only feature that distinguished the circumstances of this final, lethal morphine injection from the prior, approximately 100, nonlethal injections was the novelty of the injection environment.

There are many well-publicized cases of celebrities who suffered a fatal opiate overdose. One is struck at how often these overdoses occur in a place other than the victim's home, where presumably they usually administered the drug:[22] Sid Vicious, River Phoenix, John Belushi, Cory Monteith, and Anna Nicole Smith all suffered an overdose when they administered the drug in a novel environment. Of course, many celebrities took the fatal dose of the drug at home (Chris Farley, Philip Seymour Hoffman, Heath Ledger, Amy Winehouse), but about half of the fatal celebrity overdoses occurred in unusual environments.

Indeed, in a study of deaths in the United States between 2001 and 2020, there was a higher probability of drug overdoses in visitors, compared to residents, of US metropolitan areas.[23] It appears that taking the drug in a novel environment is a risk factor for overdose.

In addition to case reports, based on postmortem reconstructions of the events surrounding the overdose death, there is other evidence that implicates a role for the drug-administration environment in drug overdose. Not all overdose victims die. If medical assistance can be provided in a timely manner, the unconscious victim can be administered a type of drug known as an opiate antagonist. The molecules of an opiate antagonist (such as naloxone) very readily bind to opiate receptor cells in the brain. The antagonist displaces the opiate molecules from their site of action, and the toxic effect of the displaced drug is terminated. Following timely antagonist administration, the heroin overdose victim survives. Some investigators interviewed heroin overdose survivors to determine the circumstances of drug administration on the occasion of the overdose. For example, ten such survivors were located in Newark, New Jersey.[24] Detailed interviews indicated that, when they overdosed, seven of the ten respondents had self-administered the drug in circumstances that, for them, were novel. Each respondent had a different ritual associated with drug use, thus the novel administration environment was different for each of the seven who overdosed in an unusual environment. Typical is the following report of an overdose survivor:

> He "got off" with a number of other people in the living room of his house (a large crowd was present because they were celebrating the respondent's wedding earlier that day, and they used the money received as wedding gifts to purchase a quantity of heroin). According to this respondent, he, but none of the other guests

suffered an overdose after injecting from the common drug supply. This victim reported that, although he had used heroin for about 10 years, he had never before taken heroin in his living room or in such a large group.[25]

Although such reports implicating the drug-administration environment in drug overdose are intriguing, they are just anecdotes. What is the relative frequency with which addicts inject themselves in drug-associated and non-associated environments and do not suffer an overdose? An ambitious and ingenious study of heroin overdoses in Barcelona, Spain, was designed to address this question.[26] The investigators interviewed 76 heroin addicts consecutively admitted to the emergency room of a university hospital: 54 because of heroin overdose (for which they were successfully treated with an opiate antagonist), and 22 seeking urgent medical care for unrelated conditions but who had intravenously self-administered heroin one hour or less before admission (as determined by interviews and blood tests). Of the patients that had recently used heroin but did not suffer an overdose, every one had injected in an environment where they had previously used the drug. In contrast, only 48 percent of the overdose victims administered heroin in the usual environment; 52 percent injected "in an unusual setting." The different overdose frequencies in usual and unusual settings by these patients who had recently injected themselves with heroin were statistically significant (if the environment had no effect of overdose frequency, the obtained results would be expected by chance less than one time in ten thousand). As summarized by the authors, "the association between heroin overdose and unusual drug administration setting confirms the influence of non-pharmacological factors in heroin overdosing."[27]

The nonpharmacological factors relate to the setting of drug administration.

All these reports implicating the drug-administration environment in overdose are based on retrospective reports. That is, evidence is obtained following the victim's death (for example, K. J.'s death in Budapest), or from the victims' recollections after they are revived (for example, revived overdose victims in Barcelona). Conclusive evidence of a cause-and-effect relationship between the novelty of the drug-administration environment and the overdose requires prospective data. That is, to prove the importance of the environment we would need to do an experiment, in which some addicts are randomly assigned to receive a high dose of the drug in their usual drug-administration environment, and other individuals in an alternative environment. Obviously, the experiment cannot be done with people. However, it can be done, and has been done, with animals. The results of these experiments demonstrate that altering the context of drug administration does indeed increase drug-induced mortality. These experiments concerning the role of environmental cues in overdose were done at three different times, in three different countries, in three different laboratories, and using three different addictive drugs. All these independent studies demonstrated that administering the drug in a novel environment increases the risk of overdose.

There were procedural differences among these experiments, but there also were similarities. In each experiment, two groups of animals (in different experiments, rats or mice) were administered a drug on a number of occasions. On a final test session, one group was administered a high dose of the drug again, in the same environment in which it had received the prior drug administrations (Same-Tested). Another group received the test administration of the drug in an environment not previously associated with drug administration (Different-Tested). The consistent finding was that mortality was higher in Different-Tested than in Same-Tested animals. For example, in an experiment with heroin, mortality was about twice as high in Different-Tested than in Same-Tested rats.[28] Similar findings have been reported with respect to novel environmental-potentiation of death following administration of alcohol[29] and the barbiturate drug, pentobarbital.[30] Thus, results of experiments with animals are consistent with results of case reports of human overdose victims: Administering the drug to a drug-experienced organism in an environment not previously paired with drug use increases the likelihood of overdose.

Traditional risk factors explaining why addicts overdose have been extensively publicized. Some might simply take too much of the drug, especially when the heroin is enriched with even more potent opioids. Others might die because the effect of a usually sublethal dose of an opioid for these opiate-experienced individuals is enhanced by other, concomitantly administered respiratory depressive drugs, such as alcohol. Less well known is the risk of taking the drug in a novel environment—one not usually associated with drug use. The role of environmental cue novelty in overdose was not discovered until 1982.[31]

Benjamin Rush and Lawrence Kolb noted that drug-paired environmental cues precipitated drug craving, withdrawal symptoms, and relapse. These are the ghosts that haunt the addict. The overdose literature indicates that administering the drug in the presence of these usual drug-paired environmental cues can be a lifesaver. An overdose is averted. The ghost can save the addict's life. If the same drug dose is administered in a non-drug-paired environment, one that doesn't conjure the ghost and precipitate drug-withdrawal symptoms, the potential for overdose is increased.

To understand why taking the drug in a novel environment puts the addict at risk for overdose we first must understand why drug users typically do not stop breathing when they take the drug. Understanding the mechanism of survival will help us understand why this mechanism sometimes fails. Drug users do not typically suffer an overdose because, even though the drug has potent effects, their bodies have formidable mechanisms for dealing with drug-induced alterations to physiological functioning.

4 Why Addicts Usually Don't Overdose

> As a rule, whenever conditions are such as to affect the organism harmfully, factors appear within the organism itself that protect it or restore its disturbed balance.
> —Walter B. Cannon, *The Wisdom of the Body* (New York: Norton., 1932), 269

Variety may be the spice of life, but it can be deadly. Survival depends on constancy—not change. We need stability in many systems, such as concentration of various chemicals in our blood, internal temperature, blood pressure, and so on. If any of a multitude of physiological variables moves outside of a narrow range for any length of time, we get sick and then we die. We may be outside in below-zero temperature, or we may be in a sauna at 150 degrees, but our core body temperature stays constant at about 98 degrees. We may have just eaten a sugar-laden meal, or we may be declining sweets and carbohydrates, but our blood sugar concentration stays constant at about 70 to 110 milligrams per 100 milliliters. If blood pressure is too low, blood will not reach our brain; if it's too high, our blood vessels burst. Our existence is continually menaced by outside dangers, yet we manage to deal with an inhospitable environment because we have developed mechanisms to render environmental challenges ineffective. However, as we'll soon see, this very same exquisite and effective mechanism to counter environmental challenges also results in a potential for drug addiction and the complications of addiction, including overdose in a novel environment.

Claude Bernard (1813–1878) is generally given credit for initiating the study of the ways in which we maintain our internal constancy in the face of external threats. He was born in a poor family in Saint-Julien in the Beaujolais region of France (the family house is now a museum). Bernard was distracted from his early studies of pharmacy by his interest in drama, but he was not successful in his theatrical career and turned to the study of medicine. Bernard, along with his friend Louis Pasteur, eventually became the most distinguished scientists in France. Bernard championed an experimental physiology, in which hypotheses could be tested by experiments with live animals—which brought him into constant conflict with his wife, who was an avid anti-vivisectionist (the Bernards eventually separated). He became interested in what subsequently has been termed "the central problem of existence . . . the maintenance of structure and function in the face of constant internal and external assaults."[1]

Bernard discovered that we solve this "central problem of existence" not by setting up a bulwark against threats, but rather by compensating for them. We automatically detect disturbances from optimal functioning before they become large enough to be dangerous and react to these disturbances with responses that counteract them. As stated by Bernard, "far from being indifferent to the external world, the higher animal is on the contrary in a close and wise relation to it, so its equilibrium results from a continuous and delicate compensation established as if by the most sensitive of balances."[2] If we eat a sugar-laden meal our blood sugar concentration increases, but the increase in blood sugar is detected by receptors in the brain. The brain initiates responses that decrease blood sugar (primarily insulin release by the pancreas). If your blood pressure changes because of postural adjustments (e.g., moving from seated to standing), this change is detected by the brain and responses are quickly initiated to return blood pressure to normal. These responses that counter changes to our physiology occur automatically. They are the result of reflexes initiated by changes in our physiology that counter the effects of various challenges to our well-being. Just as surely as a cinder in your eye causes eyelid closure, increases in blood sugar causes insulin release.

Despite his personal fame as a physiologist, Bernard's insight that an organism's "equilibrium results from a continuous and delicate compensation established as if by the most sensitive of balances" did not have any significant influence on biological thought for over 50 years. It was Walter B. Cannon who, in 1932, made Bernard's insights central to biology.[3] The processes by which bodies achieve balance are now termed "homeostasis" (from Greek words meaning "to remain the same"). The word was neologized by Cannon (1871–1945) and discussed in his well-known book *The Wisdom of the Body*. The study of homeostasis is the study of mechanisms that are (a) initiated by threats to survival, and (b) activated to counter those threats. As succinctly summarized by Cannon: "If a state remains steady, it does so because any tendency toward change is automatically met by increased effectiveness of the factor or factors which resist the change."[4]

Taking a drug can induce a "tendency toward change." Understanding "factors which resist the change" is central to understanding addiction. Abused drugs vandalize our physiology. They disturb the activity of many chemicals in the body—chemicals that are crucial for normal communication between nerve cells. These neurochemical changes have many effects. For example, opiates cause the individual to become less sensitive to pain (analgesic effect), to decrease gastrointestinal activity (constipating effect), to suppress the cough reflex (antitussive effect), and to decrease the frequency and depth of breathing (respiratory depressive effect). It is the respiratory depressive effect that usually is responsible for opiate-induced death—the victim stops breathing. However, it is unusual for a heroin user, or a patient receiving an opiate drug, to die. How do we survive the pharmacologically induced chaos? We survive because these potential threats to survival are detected in their early stages and homeostatic counter-responses that diminish the effect of the physiological alterations are initiated. These homeostatic reflexes occur automatically and are not under voluntary control. They are part of the hard wiring in our bodies. Thus, even while an individual continues to have high levels of drug in the body and brain following drug administration, the effects of the drug decrease. Such a decrease in the effect of a drug, seen over the course of a single administration, is termed "acute tolerance." Without such acute tolerance, the drug user may not survive—rather, the individual may suffer a drug overdose.

Acute tolerance, then, results because a disturbance is detected, and responses are initiated to attenuate this disturbance before it becomes too large and dangerous. There is some lag between the time the disturbance occurs and the time the homeostatic responses are marshaled. Eventually, the drug effect wears off; the drug has been metabolized or is no longer present at receptor sites. The internal cues that initiated the homeostatic counter responses subside, as do these counter responses. Again, it takes some time before the counter responses dissipate. Thus, after a drug effect has subsided, the individual temporarily experiences the effect of the protective reflexes that were called into action by the drug effect. The individual is then said to be experiencing "drug-withdrawal symptoms." More accurately, since this example is withdrawal seen after a single administration of the drug, it is termed "acute withdrawal symptoms." For example, heroin made the individual analgesic and constipated, and had an antitussive and respiratory depressive effect. These effects were countered by homeostatic responses that had approximately the opposite effects. The individual in acute withdrawal is hypersensitive to painful stimuli, and experiences diarrhea, spontaneous coughing, and hyperventilation. These acute withdrawal symptoms may be uncomfortable, but they are necessary. They are the residual aftereffects of the homeostatic responses that are vital for survival. The acute withdrawal symptoms are the small price we pay for acute tolerance.

Homeostatic mechanisms, as described by Bernard and Cannon, are quite effective—they save our life every day of our lives. They generally function flawlessly. When an individual takes an addictive drug the drug-user usually survives. The addict, of course, does not take a drug only once; it is the repeated use of drugs that is one of the definitions of addiction. With repeated use comes enhanced tolerance. The second time a particular dose of a drug is administered it has a smaller effect than it did the first time, and the third time a smaller effect than the second time, and so on. This increased tolerance over the course of successive administrations occurs even if there is a substantial interval between the administrations (for example, days or weeks). The homeostatic machinery that decreases the effect of the drug becomes more and more effective as the drug is increasingly experienced. To distinguish the tolerance seen when a drug is first administered (that is, acute tolerance) from that seen when the drug is repeatedly administered, researchers use the term "chronic tolerance." What accounts for chronic tolerance? Why does a drug effect get smaller and smaller over the course of successive, widely spaced administrations?

When a physiologically significant event occurs over and over (like the repeated administration of heroin), a further magnificent adaptive mechanism comes into play—we learn to anticipate the event. We display homeostatic compensations for challenges prospectively, in advance of their arrival, rather than merely when they actually occur. Our tendency to anticipate threats to our well-being enormously enhances our ability to withstand such threats. On rare occasions, however, we are not well served by the anticipatory homeostasis mechanism. One such occasion occurred when K. J. died.

To understand why K. J. and other experienced drug-users who take drugs in unusual circumstances are at risk for overdose, we must appreciate the contribution of another physiologist, Ivan Petrovich Pavlov (1849–1936). It was Pavlov who first systematically studied the importance of anticipatory responses—reactions made not only in response to a physiologically significant event, but also in expectation of such an event.

5 Why Addicts Sometimes Overdose: Opiate Expectancy and Effects

> The central nervous system (CNS) anticipates present and future needs on the basis of past experience ... Error-free regulation based on experience seems to be a major achievement of the vertebrate CNS ... Truly, the body appears to be wiser than even Walter Cannon had thought.
> —George G. Somjen, "The Missing Error Signal—Regulation beyond Negative Feedback," *Physiology* 7 (1992): 184

Although both Claude Bernard and Walter Cannon made major contributions to physiology, neither received the highest accolade of that discipline—the Nobel Prize. Ivan Pavlov did win the Nobel Prize, in 1904, for his research concerning digestive physiology. He was the first Russian scientist to win the Prize. In his Nobel Prize–winning research Pavlov described the reflex pathways that are involved in extracting nutrients from food. For example, using dogs as subjects, he traced the neural pathways involved when food in the stomach elicits gastric acid secretion. In the course of these investigations Pavlov made an incidental observation that led to the research that would consume him for the last third of his career. We remember Pavlov today primarily for this latter research—an entirely new area of work that he initiated at an age when many start thinking about retirement.

In Pavlov's Nobel Prize acceptance speech, he not only discussed the gastrointestinal work that formed the basis of the award but also provided the rationale for abandoning his successful study of digestive physiology to devote his full energies to this new topic—one that he considered even more important. In his Nobel Prize–winning research, he demonstrated that digestive reflexes would occur when appropriate receptors were stimulated. However, in the course of this research, he also observed that digestive reflexes would start before the food ever reached receptors. For example, the dogs that he used in this research would display gastric acid secretion in the stomach when the food was still in its mouth. Indeed, digestive responses were noted when the dog smelled the food, saw the food, or even saw the person who normally fed it. These secretions were not reflexively elicited by food stimulating receptors in the digestive organs. They occurred when the dog expected food. They were new a type of reflex with no known neural pathway. Pavlov termed such responses "psychic" responses, to distinguish them from physiological responses. Gastric secretion, then, could occur not only in response to a physiological stimulus—food in the stomach—but also in response to psychic stimuli—stimuli that had been paired with food in the stomach, such as the sight of the food and even the sight of the food dish. Psychic responses occur in anticipation of food.

Pavlov realized the importance of these anticipatory responses. We cannot understand digestive physiology without understanding the contribution of psychic-driven secretions. For example, if Pavlov placed a piece of bread directly into the dog's stomach via a surgically implanted cannula "so as to prevent the dog from noticing it," the bread did not elicit very much gastric juice secretion: "However, when the same bread is consumed by the animal, the gastric juice secreted thereupon ... acts chemically on the protein substance of the bread, or, in more usual words, digests it."[1] More generally, psychic secretions provided a demonstration of alterations in the dog's physiology as a result of the dog's experience. It was evidence that the dog associated certain stimuli with physiologically meaningful events.

Until Pavlov, the study of how organisms form associations—how their behavior changes as a function of experience—was a topic of interest primarily to philosophers. Although some psychologists attempted to apply systematic methodology to the topic, they generally simply reflected on their own experiences as they learned something new. Pavlov realized that the study of associations could be objective and be a proper subject for a scientist. He decided to apply the methodical rigor he used to study digestive reflexes to the study of psychic processes: "Since we used the studies of the lowly organized representatives of the animal kingdom as an example, and, naturally, wanted to remain physiologists instead of becoming psychologists, we decided to take an entirely objective point of view also towards the psychical phenomena in our experiments with animals."[2]

This "objective point of view" led to a distinction between two categories of reflexes. One category consists of inborn responses. We are born with neural circuits that cause certain stimuli to invariably produce certain responses. These stimuli trigger brain activity that causes reflexive responses to occur. A cinder in the eye causes tearing, heat applied to a limb causes withdrawal of that limb, dry food in the mouth causes salivation, and food in the stomach causes secretion of gastric acid.

Pavlov termed these "unconditional reflexes" or "unconditional responses." That is, they are elicited unconditionally—every time receptor cells detect the appropriate stimulus (the "unconditional stimulus"), the sensory information is transmitted to the central nervous system, where neural activity is initiated, resulting in the observed reflex response. Pavlov realized that an arbitrary stimulus that has been paired with an unconditional stimulus a sufficient number of times would also elicit a reflex response. Thus, psychic secretion was an example of a reflex response that was not unconditional, but rather, was conditional on the animals' history of having certain stimuli (for example, the sight of the food dish) reliably paired with food in the stomach. Although he originally termed these reflexes elicited by previously neutral stimuli that had been paired with unconditional stimuli "psychic reflexes," Pavlov later came to label these acquired reflexes "conditional reflexes," or "conditional responses." Their occurrence was conditional on the animal's experience. Inborn reflexes are sometimes referred to as "uncondition*ed* reflexes" (rather than "uncondition*al* reflexes") and acquired reflexes as "condition*ed* reflexes" (rather than "condition*al* reflexes"). The use of the terms "unconditioned" and "conditioned" is due to a translation error in Pavlov's writings.[3]

Conditional responses, like unconditional responses, are automatic. Just as we are compelled to make an unconditional response if we are presented with the unconditional stimulus, we are compelled to make a conditional response if we are presented with the conditional stimulus, a previously neutral stimulus that has been paired with the unconditional stimulus. The organism that has been subject to Pavlovian conditioning doesn't have to be consciously aware of the pairing of conditional and unconditional stimulus to display a conditional response.

During the last 35 years of his life Pavlov studied the rules that determined the strengthening and weakening of conditional reflexes. Although Pavlov was nominated for a second Nobel Prize on four subsequent occasions between 1925 and 1930 for this conditional-reflex research, he did not receive the award a second time.[4]

Pavlov set about to systematically study the associations between stimuli that had been paired with the effects of the food. It was difficult to present natural food-predictive cues, such as the sight of the food dish (difficult to turn on and off), and to study gastric secretions (required extensive surgery). To study these associations with appropriate scientific rigor, he set up a laboratory in which dogs could be presented with precisely controlled arbitrary stimuli (sounds, light, tactile stimulation) shortly before they were presented with dry food. A dog, like a person, reflexively secretes saliva when receptors in the mouth are stimulated by dry food, and the procedure to measure salivation was minimally invasive. Thus, this foray into the topic of what is now called Pavlovian conditioning involved the measurement of salivation.

In the archetypical Pavlovian conditioning procedure, the dog was presented on several occasions with a neutral stimulus, such as a tone, shortly before it was presented with the dry food. The dry food in the mouth acts as an unconditional stimulus. It unconditionally elicits a homeostatic response (the unconditional response or unconditional reflex), salivation, which compensates for the dry mouth. An arbitrary stimulus (a tone, in this example) is the conditional stimulus. Conditional on its pairing with the dry mouth, the tone comes to elicit salivation.

A new reflex—a conditional reflex—has been established. Quoting Pavlov, "the activity of the salivary gland has thus been called into play by impulses of sound—a stimulus quite alien to food."[5] The same observation of conditional salivation could be obtained if the unconditional salivary reflex was initiated by weak acid infused into the dog's mouth. The salivation compensates for the acidic stimulation by diluting the acid. In fact, a variety of different unconditional reflexes can be paired with a conditional stimulus, and the reflex will come to be seen in response to the conditional stimulus.

Coincidently, shortly before the time that Pavlov initiated his studies of the conditional salivary reflex in Russia, a graduate student at the University of Pennsylvania, Edward B. Twitmeyer, completed his doctoral research investigating the patellar tendon reflex (the knee jerk reflex). In his thesis, completed in 1902, he investigated the reflex by sounding a warning bell half a second before striking the tendon. All his subjects eventually displayed involuntary knee jerks to the bell before the tendon was struck.[6] Twitmeyer did not continue this work on anticipatory responding, and his thesis research was largely unrecognized in his lifetime (he died in 1943). His landmark contribution was not published until 1974 in the *Journal of Experimental Psychology*.

For whatever reason, the discovery of conditional responses is attributable to Pavlov, rather than Twitmeyer. Pavlov realized that he was studying something far more important than salivation in response to environmental stimuli. He was studying the formation of associations. Conditional salivation was simply a convenient index of association formation, and generally was relevant to understanding the laws by which conditional reflexes are formed. If two events are presented closely in time, a neutral conditional stimulus followed by a biologically significant unconditional stimulus, they will become automatically associated. The procedure is known as Pavlovian conditioning. The response reflexively elicited by the unconditional stimulus will come to be elicited in anticipation of the unconditional stimulus. Without the necessity of any conscious awareness of the pairing, we are compelled to prepare for a biological event (the unconditional stimulus) if we have a history of a neutral stimulus (the conditional stimulus) being paired with the unconditional stimulus.

Consider, for example, the effects of a drug. Like the effects of food, drug effects are not typically experienced in isolation. Rather, typically there are stimuli that are uniquely present at the time the drug effect occurs, and not present when the drug effect does not occur. Pavlov recognized that the administration of a drug could be viewed as a conditioning trial; the drug effect serves as the unconditional stimulus and the surrounding environmental cues serve as conditional stimuli. As previously discussed, prior to any learning, many drug effects reflexively elicit homeostatic unconditional responses—responses that compensate for the drug-induced disturbances and that account for acute tolerance. After some drug administrations, homeostatic responses occur in the presence of drug-administration cues. Such learned responses have been termed *conditional homeostatic responses*. Conditional homeostatic responses have been demonstrated with respect to many effects of a variety of drugs, including commonly used drugs such as alcohol, caffeine, nicotine, and opiates such as heroin. That is, when presented with stimuli that previously have been paired with these drugs, people and animals respond with homeostatic compensatory responses that normally are elicited by these drugs even when the drug is not actually administered.[7] To paraphrase Pavlov, the homeostatic responses initiated by drugs have thus been called into play by cues present at the time of drug administration—environmental stimuli quite alien to drug effects.

The conditional homeostatic response—the response elicited by drug-associated cues—is the ghost in the addict. The conditional homeostatic response is what protects the addict from overdose.

Our response to many drugs, then, is really a combination of the direct drug effect and conditional homeostatic responses that are made in anticipation of the drug effect. We counteract the dangerous effects of the forthcoming drug when we are in the presence of stimuli that have been paired with the drug in the past. These conditional homeostatic responses get bigger and bigger as the drug is paired more and more often with the usual drug-predictive cues. In other words, when we expect a drug (because we are in the presence of cues that, in the past, have signaled the imminent arrival of the drug in our body), we respond in ways that will mitigate the effect of the drug.

As demonstrated by Pavlov and many others, conditional reflexes in general, and conditional reflexes based on drugs in particular, are very well retained. That is, they do not diminish very much merely as a function of the passage of time. Even after a drug-free period, if an individual again administers the drug in the usual setting, he or she will again display the learned compensation for the drug effect in anticipation of the actual drug delivery. Although the drug user likely is unaware that he or she has actually learned about the relationship between drug-paired cues and the effect of the drug, this learned compensation is a major mechanism of chronic drug tolerance.[8]

The previously described cases of K. J. in Budapest, the cancer patient, N. E., in Pennsylvania who overdosed on medically prescribed morphine, and the overdose survivors in Newark and Barcelona, along with the results of experiments with animals, all indicate that the drug-experienced organism is at risk for overdose when a high dose of the drug is administered in the context of stimuli that have not, in the past, reliably been paired with the drug. These victims did not make the conditional homeostatic responses that are responsible for chronic tolerance because the drug was administered in the presence of cues that had not previously been associated with the drug effect. On the occasion of the overdose, these people (and animals) were simply not tolerant to the drug.

There is evidence that learned responses to drug-paired cues affect tolerance to the lethal effects of a variety of drugs. For example, some Brazilian researchers described the role of conditional response in cocaine overdose:

> A cocaine dependent person knows how many "bags" they can sniff to achieve behavioral arousal. As he or she goes to the usual place of consumption (bar, club etc.), their body gradually prepares itself, through anticipatory responses, for the drug to enter the organism, and "craving" increases. However, if cocaine is presented outside their usual consumption environment (for example, in the workplace) which had not been associated with use, the commonly consumed amount will have a much greater effect than the intended familiar one, thus causing overdose with serious risks. This is because the stimuli that compose the work environment do not have the power to elicit the compensatory effects of the drug in anticipation.[9]

As recently summarized by some noted addiction researchers, "individuals with OUD [Opioid Use Disorder] are especially susceptible to overdose death when they use opioids in unfamiliar contexts or with unfamiliar cues . . . and their bodies fail to engage learned compensatory mechanisms."[10] In an unfamiliar context, there is no summoning of the ghost that protects the addict from overdose. Although the evidence implicating environmental cues in overdose is overwhelming, there is not yet wide dissemination of this information, either among clinicians who treat patients with opiates for pain relief or clinicians who deal with heroin addicts or other addicted individuals. The report of K. J.'s overdose was published in 2005; K. J. died in 1999—the same year that a prominent overdose researcher, Deborah Zador, commented on potential mechanisms of heroin overdose. She noted, "ingesting heroin in an unusual or unfamiliar setting is not currently publicized as a risk."[11] Unfortunately, that's still true, although the conditioning interpretation of heroin overdose was described in a work of fiction also published in 1999, when Marion Chesney (using the pseudonym "M. C. Beaton") wrote *Death of an Addict*. It was one of the novels featuring the clever but unambitious Scottish Highlands bobby, Hamish Macbeth. In the novel, the pathologist knows of the conditioning interpretation of overdose:

> Dr. Sinclair leaned his cadaverous body against his car and settled down to give a lecture. "The reason for tolerance to heroin is partially conditioned by the environment where the drug was normally administered. If the drug is administered in a new setting, much of the conditioned tolerance will disappear and the addict will be more likely to overdose."[12]

Although the conditioning interpretation of overdose was recognized in fiction in 1999, it still is not currently part of drug education of drug addicts. If heroin users (and likely other drug users, too) knew of the risk of administering the drug in a new environment, lives would be saved.

Although administering the drug in a novel environment is a risk factor in overdose, sometimes the drug-user will overdose even when the drug is administered in the usual drug-administration environment. When the drug is an exceptionally high dose, augmented by very potent synthetic opioids (such as fentanyl), the addict might very well overdose wherever he or she is taking the drug. The drug dose can be so great that it overwhelms the addict's tolerance. The high dose is due to the illegal status of drug administration; the addict must take what the illicit market supplies. When there are few legal restrictions concerning drug use, and the addict is not at the mercy of illicit sources of the drug, overdose is not common. In the nineteenth-century era of free and legal opiate availability, accidental adult deaths due to opiates were not substantial.[13] After the passage of the Harrison Narcotics Act, medically supervised morphine maintenance clinics were established in the 1920s to deal with the especially intractable newly criminalized opiate addicts. Overdoses were not a problem in these clinics. The largest opiate maintenance clinic was in Shreveport, Louisiana. In the study of the Shreveport clinic, it was noted that "there were never problems with overdose,"[14] even though these maintenance patients self-administered very large morphine doses. Overdoses generally occur when addicts unknowingly take a large dose of the drug (because they must rely on whatever the illegal market supplies), especially if he or she administers the drug in a novel environment.

Understanding the importance of the novelty of the drug-administration environment as a risk factor in overdose is due primarily to the homeostasis research of Walter Cannon and the conditioning research of Ivan Pavlov. These two men were friends and colleagues, but they never referenced each other's research. It remained for subsequent researchers to realize that they were both engaged in related activities.

6 Ivan P. Pavlov, Walter B. Cannon, and Homeostasis

> Cannon and Pavlov were close friends, and when Pavlov came to America, he stayed with the Cannons in a house on Divinity Avenue.
> —Burrhus F. Skinner, "Some Responses to the Stimulus 'Pavlov,'" *Conditional Reflex: A Pavlovian Journal of Research & Therapy* 1, no. 2 (1996): 74

Most physiological disturbances unconditionally reflexively elicit homeostatic responses that counteract the unconditional stimulus. These unconditional reflexes were studied by Walter Cannon. If the unconditional reflex occurs over and over following the same environmental stimuli, they come to be conditionally elicited by these stimuli that are paired with the disturbance. These conditional reflexes, which enhance the unconditional homeostatic reflex, were studied by Ivan Pavlov.

Pavlov had a substantial reputation in America, and Walter Cannon became Pavlov's friend and colleague. In 1920 Cannon discovered that Pavlov had difficulty obtaining food in St. Petersburg due to the famine created by the Russian Civil War. Cannon worked to get financial assistance to Pavlov, and Cannon and Pavlov began a corresponding relationship and friendship. Pavlov made his first trip to North America in 1923, and he visited Cannon in Cambridge, Massachusetts. Pavlov made the trip with his son, Vladimir (who was fluent in English and served as his translator). When Ivan and Vladimir boarded a train at Grand Central Terminal in New York City on their way to visit Cannon, they were mugged and robbed of all their funds. The Rockefeller Institute then supported the Pavlovs for the remainder of their trip.[1] Cannon and Pavlov met again in 1929, when Pavlov attended the International Physiological Congress in Boston, and in 1935, in Leningrad, at another meeting of the International Physiological Congress.

Pavlov lamented the fact that his work did not sufficiently influence physiological thought. In 1935, at one of his regular laboratory meetings, he commented: "Strange as it may seem, many physiologists, authors of textbooks, do not cite any data concerning our experiments with conditioned reflexes."[2] Surprisingly, this was even true of books and papers written by Walter Cannon.

For Cannon, homeostatic responses were reflexively generated in response to a perturbation, and these responses reduced the perturbation. This is a simple negative feedback view of homeostasis. Initially there was no realization that the homeostatic response could get bigger as it was repeatedly exercised. It took many years to realize that homeostatic corrections for physiological disturbances often became more pronounced the more often they occurred.

In 1974 two psychologists, Richard Solomon and John Corbit, noted that compensatory responses elicited by physiological disturbances can get bigger as they are repeatedly initiated, and can increasingly cancel the disturbance that initiates the compensatory response. Solomon and Corbit labeled the response directly caused by the physiological disturbance the "A" response, and the reflex that compensated for the A response the "B" response. They didn't label the compensatory B response a homeostatic response, but it's clear from their article that that's what it was. For example, the analgesic effect of morphine (decreased pain sensitivity) becomes weaker and weaker over the course of successive morphine administrations because the compensatory response elicited by morphine (in this example, hyperalgesia, or increased sensitivity to painful stimuli) becomes stronger and stronger. For Solomon and Corbit, however, this growth of the compensatory response was not due to learning. According to them, "the person repeatedly dosed with morphine does not have to know anything and is not required to be subjected to Pavlovian stimulus contingencies."[3] The homeostatic response simply grew in strength as it was repeatedly exercised, much like a muscle grows stronger as it is repeatedly exercised. Solomon and Corbit's view of homeostatic response strengthening over repeated elicitations merely as a result of it being exercised was challenged one year later. In 1975 evidence was presented demonstrating that the growth of the homeostatic response over repeated elicitations was not due simply to exercise-induced strengthening, but rather to Pavlovian conditioning. The more robust homeostatic response seen with repeated administrations was seen only if the biologically significant unconditional stimulus was administered repeatedly in the presence of the same cues: "the direct analgesic effect of morphine becomes attenuated over the course of successive administrations of the narcotic by a conditioned, compensatory, hyperalgesic response [increased pain sensitivity] elicited by the administration procedure, the net result being analgesic tolerance."[4]

In the explanation of Pavlovian conditioning and drug tolerance that was first elucidated in 1975, the conditional response elicited by drug-paired stimuli was hypothesized to be opposite in direction to the drug response. For example, morphine caused analgesia, and the conditional response was hyperalgesia. In retrospect, this older analysis of drug conditioning confused the unconditional stimulus and the unconditional response. We now know that the analgesic effect of morphine is the unconditional stimulus, *not* the unconditional response. The analgesic effect is due to the drug's direct stimulation of receptor cells in the brain. Activity in these cells causes the brain to reflexively initiate homeostatic responses that compensate for the direct effect of the drug. These unconditionally elicited compensatory responses are responsible for acute tolerance. After some pairings of the drug-paired conditional stimulus and the drug-induced unconditional stimulus, the drug-compensatory responses are elicited as conditioned responses. As noted by neuroscientist and psychologist Barry Dworkin, this analysis now closely follows Pavlov's conceptualization of conditioning: "Conditioned drug responses, when adequately isolated, dissected, and understood, exemplify in an uncomplicated way the phenomenon first described by Pavlov: The conditioned reflex resembles the unconditioned reflex, and as it develops, it augments the effect of the unconditioned reflex."[5]

Pavlov did not incorporate homeostatic concepts in his conditioning work, and Cannon did not recognize that homeostatic responses might be seen in anticipation of the perturbation. Early attempts to integrate the work of the two scientists were largely ignored. For example, in 1938 (just two years after Pavlov's death and seven years before Cannon's death), psychologist Elmer Culler asserted that the function of the conditional response was "to make preparatory adjustments for an oncoming stimulus.... The CR [conditional response], in brief, is nature's way of getting ready for an important stimulus."[6] Culler's insight had little effect. It was only much later that the role of the conditional response in anticipatory homeostasis was generally recognized. In the words of addiction researchers Douglas Ramsay and Stephen Woods:

> If negative feedback were the only mechanism that existed, regulation would be a sluggish and highly inefficient process. A physiological insult great enough to trigger a reflexive response would have to already exist before regulation was initiated. The body would thus have to dedicate considerable resources (time and energy) to putting out fires, as it were. Luckily, that's not how most regulation works. Converging research over the past few decades has revealed that it is preferable, and indeed more common, for organisms to take advantage of past experiences to enable them to prepare for potential challenges and ameliorate them before they occur, i.e., an underappreciated mechanism for achieving physiological regulation is anticipatory responding, which allows for better compensation or preparedness for an impending physiologically relevant stimulus.[7]

The study of "anticipatory responding" is the study of Pavlovian conditioning.

As pointed out by Barry Dworkin, "he [Cannon] failed entirely to appreciate the far-reaching implications for homeostasis of the extraordinary experiments and brilliant insights of his personal friend Ivan Pavlov."[8] It is also true that Pavlov largely failed to appreciate the role of the conditional response in homeostasis. Unfortunately, the Cannon–Pavlov correspondence has been lost,[9] and we are left with an enigma. These men, although friends and colleagues, apparently had little intellectual effect on each other.

7 Learning and Drug Tolerance

> Learning is the primary underlying cause of the development of drug tolerance.
> —Douglas S. Ramsay and Stephen C. Woods, "Biological Consequences of Drug Administration: Implications for Acute and Chronic Tolerance," *Psychological Review* 104, no. 1 (1997): 170

The physiological insult produced by a drug is minimized by the conditional responses made in the presence of drug-paired cues before the actual drug effect (the unconditional stimulus) is experienced. The unconditional response is a reflex that automatically is elicited by activity in the central nervous system in response to the unconditional stimulus. If we are eating a sugar-laden meal (or if, in an experiment, animals or humans are injected with sugar), the concentration of sugar in the blood increases. That is the unconditional stimulus. The high–blood sugar concentration is detected by receptors in the brain, which reflexively signal the pancreas to release insulin (which lowers blood sugar concentration). Insulin release is the unconditional response and will also eventually occur as a conditional response. In Pavlov's original research the dry food caused a dry mouth. The dry mouth is the unconditional stimulus that is detected by cells in the brain, and saliva is reflexively released—the unconditional response. Salivation eventually occurs as the conditional response.

The role of drug-paired cues in tolerance is clearly evidenced by the role of these cues in overdose. In the overdose situation there often is a failure of tolerance to occur because the usual drug-paired cues are absent. When these cues are present, the usual drug-paired stimuli call forth the ghost of drugs past. The conditional drug response occurs. It is this conditional response that often saves the addicts' life following self-administration of a large drug dose administered in the usual administration environment. The learning resulting from the pairing of drug-administered cues with the effects of the drug is adaptive—it is responsible for chronic drug tolerance.

In addition, there are many experiments, conducted mainly with animals, that provide convincing evidence that tolerance depends on the occurrence of the usual drug-paired cues when the drug is experienced. For example, there are numerous demonstrations, in addition to the overdose literature, that drug tolerance is environmentally specific. If individuals have been made tolerant to a drug in one environment, administering the drug in another environment results in a nontolerant response. The environmental specificity of tolerance has been demonstrated with respect to tolerance to many effects of a variety of drugs. Environmental specificity of tolerance has also been demonstrated with nicotine[1] and caffeine,[2] in addition to the opiates and alcohol studies. The finding has been reported by clinicians, epidemiologists, and laboratory scientists.[3] It has been observed in many species, from snails to humans, suggesting (according to the addiction researchers, Martin Kavaliers and Maurice Hirst) that such specificity "may be a general phenomenon having an early evolutionary development and broad phylogenetic continuity."[4]

Prior to recognizing that tolerance is due to Pavlovian conditioning, most thought that a history of drug administration was sufficient to confer tolerance. An individual who experienced a drug on many occasions was considered likely to be tolerant. Early interpretations of tolerance did not ascribe any role to learning.[5] Some theorists proposed that the experience with the drug altered the drug-taker's metabolism—that the drug is more efficiently metabolized. Other theorists proposed that the drug receptors became desensitized to the drug as they were increasingly stimulated by repeated administrations of the drug. Still others have suggested that tolerance is the result of an immune response to the drug.[6] According to all these explanations of tolerance, experience with the drug is sufficient to confer a weakened response to the drug. We now know that the answer to the question about whether a drug-experienced individual is tolerant is more subtle. The correct answer is, "it depends." "It depends" on whether the drug-experienced individual is tested in the context of the usual drug-paired cues (in which case tolerance is demonstrated) or tested in the presence of novel cues (in which case tolerance is not demonstrated). Thus, the same individual with a history of drug administration displays both a tolerant response and a nontolerant response, a small drug effect and a large drug effect, depending on the environment in which testing occurs.

What if there are ever-changing stimuli presented prior to drug administration? In that case, tolerance should be slowed down because there is no opportunity for reliable drug-paired stimuli to be paired with the drug. In an experiment by nicotine researchers Leonard Epstein and colleagues, male, college-age participants puffed on a cigarette for five sessions. The cigarette was paired with segments of a Sherlock Holmes radio show. The same segment was repeatedly paired with the cigarette for one group (Repeated Segment), while different, successive segments of the show were paired with the cigarette for another group (Changing Segment). The effect of the cigarette on heart rate was monitored. Smoking caused an elevation in heart rate, but tolerance across the five smoking sessions quickly developed for the Repeated Segment group; the elevation level in heart rate decreased over smoking sessions. Smoking-induced increases in heart rate showed much less tolerance for the Changing Segment group. As expected by a Pavlovian conditioning interpretation of tolerance, there was little tolerance seen over repeated drug administrations if the cue that was paired with the drug was unreliable.[7]

Pavlov studied not only manipulations that led to an increase in the magnitude of conditional responses but also manipulations that led to a decrease in the magnitude of established conditional responses. When the dog was conditioned to display salivation to a tone that had been paired with dry food, it would gradually fail to exhibit this conditional response if tone presentation were no longer accompanied by food. The procedure is termed "extinction."[8] *Extinction* consists of presenting the conditional stimulus many times, but not presenting the usual unconditional stimulus with which the conditional stimulus had been paired.

Tolerance to the analgesic, lethal, and behavioral sedating effects of morphine are attenuated by repeated presentations of drug-paired cues (i.e., engaging in the usual drug administration ritual but administering an inert substance, such as physiological saline, rather than the drug). Similarly, tolerance to a variety of effects of alcohol, amphetamine, and midazolam (a short-acting benzodiazepine) can be extinguished.[9] A seemingly innocuous treatment, repeated administrations of an inert substance, can reverse established tolerance—a result not explicable by interpretations of tolerance that do not incorporate Pavlovian conditioning principles.

Pavlovian conditioning can be retarded by disrupting brain activity after each conditioning trial. Thus, if after each trial the animal is subject to high-voltage electric shocks to the brain (electroconvulsive shock, or ECS), or low-voltage stimulation of certain brain regions, the development of the conditional response is disrupted. These manipulations also disrupt the development of drug tolerance. As summarized by addiction researchers Raymond Kesner and colleagues, "the data from both the ECS and discrete brain stimulation experiments provide additional support for a possible parallel between conventional learning and tolerance to drugs."[10]

The expression of conditional responses is disrupted by a distracting stimulus. The phenomenon is termed "external inhibition," and was described by Pavlov in the salivary conditioning situation:

> The dog and the experimenter would be isolated in the experimental room, all the conditions remaining for a while constant. Suddenly some disturbing factor would arise—a sound would penetrate the room; some quick change in illumination would occur, the sun going behind a cloud; or a draught would get in underneath the door, and maybe bring some odour with it. If any of these extra stimuli happened to be introduced just at the time of application of the conditioned stimulus, it would inevitably bring about a more or less pronounced weakening or even a complete disappearance of the reflex response depending on the strength of the extra stimulus.[11]

There are several demonstrations that, as expected on the basis of a conditioning interpretation of tolerance, when a rat is displaying a small, tolerant response to a drug (because it is administered the drug in the usual drug-administration environment), presentation of a distracting stimulus causes a sudden appearance of a large, nontolerant response.[12] Indeed, the ability of a novel event to obliterate tolerance may be relevant to some instances of drug overdose:

> The conditioning analysis of tolerance has shown to be important in understanding drug overdose. . . . Based on findings of external inhibition of tolerance, we would predict that if people consistently administer a drug under one set of circumstances, a novel stimulus presentation or the novel omission of a stimulus should disrupt tolerance and result in an exaggerated drug effect.[13]

In fact, there is a case report in which external inhibition of tolerance may have contributed to a heroin overdose.[14] The victim (E. C.) was a heavy user of heroin for three years. She usually self-administered her first daily dose of heroin in the bathroom of her apartment, where she lived with her mother. Typically, E. C. would awake earlier than her mother, turn on the water in the bathroom (pretending to take a shower) and self-inject without arousing suspicion. However, on the occasion of the overdose her mother was already awake when E. C. started her injection ritual, and her mother knocked loudly on the bathroom door telling E. C. to hurry. When E. C. then injected the heroin, she immediately found that she could not breathe. She was unable to call to her mother for help (her mother eventually broke down the bathroom door and rushed E. C. to the hospital, where she was successfully treated for heroin overdose). It is likely that the novel, external stimulus (mother knocking loudly on the bathroom door) disrupted the drug-preparatory response usually elicited by drug-associated cues.

The disruption of tolerance by a novel stimulus may have forensic implications. Assume someone has self-administered a drug in the usual administration environment, and thus is tolerant to the drug administered in this environment. The usual drug-administration environment might be, for example, the addict's car. According to the psychologist Traci Rieckmann, "if you habitually use [the drug] in your car, for example, the body prepares itself to receive the drug when it is in that environment."[15] The tolerance might disappear (the drug effect may be enhanced) by the sudden appearance of a novel stimulus, such as the arrival of the police while the drug-user is in the car.[16]

Chronic tolerance results because people prepare for a drug in anticipation of its arrival. Stimuli that have come to predict a drug effect elicit homeostatic drug responses. What happens if there are no drug-predictive stimuli? Consider the situation in which rats live in a homogeneous dark and quiet environment. Occasionally they are presented with a distinctive audio-visual stimulus, and occasionally they receive a morphine injection. The distinctive stimulus is paired with the morphine injection for some rats (Paired Group), and not paired with the morphine injection for other rats (Unpaired Group). After a number of stimulus presentations and morphine administrations, in test sessions all rats receive the drug following the distinctive cue and analgesia is assessed. In an experiment using this procedure, Paired Group rats, but not Unpaired Group rats, displayed tolerance in the test. The pre-test morphine administrations, which were not paired with the distinctive cues, did not result in tolerance when rats were tested in the presence of these cues.[17]

There is an even more surprising finding from research inspired by the conditioning analysis of tolerance. It should actually be possible to retard the development of morphine tolerance by administering the drug. Imagine rats living in a dark, homogeneous environment receive a distinctive audio/

visual cue from time to time, and also receive an injection of morphine from time to time, but the cue always signals a long period free of the drug. The animals should learn that the distinctive cue means that they will not get morphine. When these rats subsequently received morphine in the presence of this cue, their learning to associate this cue with the drug was hindered—they were slow to develop tolerance to morphine.[18] The fact that a procedure that involves morphine administration can retard the development of tolerance is explicable only by the conditioning interpretation of tolerance.

There is an overwhelming amount of research, conducted primarily with rats, that indicates there are parallels between learning and morphine tolerance. In fact, drug expectancy not only affects our response to opiate drugs, but to non-opiate drugs as well. It certainly contributes to our responsiveness to a leading non-opiate addictive drug in our culture—alcohol. This conclusion was originally seen as unwarranted extension of animal research findings to humans. According to Ray Hodgson, a noted British alcohol researcher, an alcoholic who is tolerant to alcohol in the usual drinking environment would not inevitably lose that tolerance if they drank alcohol in a novel environment:

> Of course, we must not take the animal analogues too literally. For example, we should not expect situational factors to be quite as strong in human drug dependence. It is very unlikely that an alcoholic who feels only slight intoxication after four doubles would be legless if he consumed the same amount on Ilkley Moor.[19]

Nobody has assessed whether situational specificity of alcohol tolerance would be displayed by testing the alcoholic in a novel environment on a moor in West Yorkshire. However, there is a considerable amount of evidence that conditioning contributes to tolerance to alcohol, both in humans and animals.

8   Alcohol Expectancy and Alcohol's Effect

> Somebody should do a study, he thought, about why drinks in the afternoon hit so much harder than they did at night. It was one of life's profound mysteries.
>
> —John Lescroart, *Poison* (New York: Atria Books, 2018), 10

Suppose you usually have a pre-dinner cocktail at the end of a busy day. You relax at home and have a martini. You enjoy the ritual and do not think that the drink makes you particularly intoxicated. You do not normally drink at other times during the working day. However, one day you are eating lunch with coworkers and, uncharacteristically, order a drink. Much to your surprise you find that you feel the effects of the alcohol.

A 2023 article in the *New York Times* was devoted to elaborating the greater intoxicating effect of daytime drinking compared to evening drinking.[1] The author attempted to answer the question, "Why does a daytime buzz feel different from after-dinner drinks?" The "psychiatrists and alcohol experts" interviewed for the article offered several hypotheses but did not recognize the primary reason for the greater effect of daytime alcohol. Alcohol has a greater intoxicating effect when it is consumed at an unusual time because the cues at this time are different from the cues that are usually paired with alcohol consumption. The novel drinking cues do not elicit an alcohol-compensatory response that dulls the effects of the drug.

This common observation that drinking at an unusual time causes greater intoxication than drinking at the usual time has been confirmed in the laboratory. The subjects were medical student volunteers who reported that they usually did their social drinking in the evening. When they consumed a measured amount of alcohol in the laboratory they demonstrated more impairment when they drank it in the afternoon than when they drank it in the evening. The authors provided a compensatory homeostatic conditioning interpretation of their findings: "Most subjects were accustomed to drinking in the evening and had 'learned' to compensate for the deleterious effects of alcohol. Thus, drinking alcohol in the afternoon may be a very different 'experience' from drinking it in the evening."[2]

There have been many experiments designed to evaluate the effects of alcohol-associated stimuli on alcohol tolerance. It is much easier to study the effects of environmental stimuli on tolerance to a legal drug, like alcohol, than an illegal drug, like heroin. People will readily volunteer to participate in experiments in which they get to drink experimenter-provided alcohol. There are many laboratory experiments demonstrating that Pavlovian conditioning influences tolerance to alcohol in the same way that it influences tolerance to opiates.[3] For example, in one experiment, reported in 1986,[4] male volunteers drank an alcohol-tonic mixture in a distinctive environment five times (once every other day). On the alternate days when they did not drink the alcohol beverage, the subjects drank plain tonic. Each beverage was presented in the context of different environmental cues. In the "Lab" environment, the beverage was offered in a large room filled with a variety of laboratory paraphernalia. To make this Lab environment even more distinctive, just before drinking the beverage in this environment the participants were asked to gargle with a green, menthol-flavored mouthwash. The alternative "Home" environment was set up as a small bedroom, equipped with a television, bed, dresser, table, and chair. In the Home environment, too, a distinctive feature was added—prior to consuming the beverage in the Home environment, participants gargled with a red, cherry-flavored mouthwash. One half the participants consumed the alcohol-tonic mixture in the Lab environment, and the unadulterated tonic in the Home environment. For the other half of the participants, presentation of the environmental cues and substances ingested were reversed. Finally, in a test session, all participants consumed the tonic-alcohol mixture in the Lab environment and were given a test to measure alcohol-induced cognitive impairment. Prior to this test all participants had equal experience drinking alcohol (and tonic) in the experiment, and they were equally familiar with the two distinctive environments. Nevertheless, in the test in the Lab environment, those who had previously consumed alcohol in this environment were less impaired than were those who consumed alcohol in the Home environment. Similar results were reported in 2011 in an experiment studying both men and women college students.[5]

One advantage of using alcohol in studies of the effects of drug-predictive stimuli is that routine alcohol use is inherently paired with a variety of such stimuli. If a study uses social drinkers, they do not have to be trained in an experiment to associate certain locations or flavors with the drug effect. Such pairings have already taken place before the participant enters the study, and this pre-experimental history can be exploited in the laboratory experiment. For example, much research is done with university-student volunteers. It is not difficult to find, in this population, a lot of people who routinely drink beer in a pub. Prior to participating in any experiment they have already been subjected to Pavlovian conditioning; they have experienced many pairings of a particular flavor (beer) and environmental context (pub setting) with the systemic effects of alcohol. These cues should elicit conditional homeostatic responses. One might hypothesize that these people should be more tolerant to alcohol presented in their usual flavored form and usual context than to the same amount of alcohol presented in an alternative manner. An experiment to evaluate this prediction was conducted in 1990 by Christopher McCusker and Kia Brown.[6] All the participants were undergraduates at Queens University in Belfast, Northern Ireland, and were social drinkers (consuming, on average, about one-half pint of beer per day). They were divided into groups. One group was given alcohol in a familiar form and context (they consumed beer in a simulated pub), while a second group was administered the same dose of alcohol in a novel form and unusual context (the alcohol was mixed in artificially sweetened carbonated water and consumed in an office setting). Based on several objective measures of intoxication, the novel context group became more inebriated than the familiar context group.

McCusker and Brown evaluated the effects of context by manipulating both external stimuli (the place where the alcohol was consumed) and stimuli inherent to the beverage (the flavor of the drink). In fact, it is possible to demonstrate the situational-specificity of alcohol tolerance merely by manipulating flavor, as was demonstrated in an experiment reported in 1997. The participants were students at Southampton University in England.[7] All the participants drank an alcoholic beverage prior to assessment of alcohol-induced impairment on a variety of tasks. For some participants, the alcohol was presented in the context of a familiar flavor—beer (familiar drink group). For the other participants, the same amount of alcohol was presented in a novel colored and flavored beverage—a blue, peppermint-flavored drink (unfamiliar drink group). Even though both groups consumed the same amount of alcohol, the familiar drink group was significantly less intoxicated (that is, more tolerant) than the unfamiliar drink group.

The results obtained from the Southampton University students were confirmed 13 years later in a study using students from the University of Birmingham in England. Perhaps there is some propensity for students from the United Kingdom to routinely drink a lot, and to prefer beer as their alcoholic beverage, thus making them especially suitable for displaying heightened intoxication after consuming alcohol in something other than beer. The Birmingham students were tested for alcohol-induced impairment after drinking a glass of alcohol-enriched beer, or the same amount of alcohol in what was, for these participants, a nontraditional, fruit-flavored beverage. Impairment was assessed with a computerized battery of neuropsychological tests designed to assess "executive functioning." These tests measured the ability to follow complicated instructions, to alter responding when presented with new rules, and to respond as quickly as possible. The results indicated significantly less impairment in participants that consumed their alcohol in a beer-flavored beverage than in participants that consumed their alcohol in the unusually flavored drinks. The authors concluded: "These findings suggest that consumption of alcohol in the absence of cues usually associated with alcohol's effects—for example, in a very novel drink format—may disrupt executive functioning, which might place the drinker at heightened risk of mishap."[8] This "heightened risk of mishap" may be relevant to understanding unusual problems with alcohol that have been seen on several university campuses.

In 2010 and 2011 many university administrators notified their students to beware of a new, highly intoxicating alcoholic beverage that was legal and widely available. In September 2010, 23 students at Ramapo College in Mahwah, New Jersey, were hospitalized for alcohol intoxication. The next month, after a party in Ellensburg, Washington, attended by Central Washington State College students, 12 partygoers had to be hospitalized for acute alcohol intoxication. About that time a spokesperson for Bellevue Hospital in New York City noted a spike in emergency-room admissions of young people suffering from severe alcohol poisoning. A beverage named Four Loko was identified as the culprit in these (and many other) cases of widespread and severe alcohol intoxication. Four Loko has been labeled "blackout in a can" and "liquid cocaine." Phusion Projects, the manufacturer of Four Loko, has been a defendant in several unlawful death lawsuits.

Three students at Ohio State University invented Four Loko in 2005. The product they developed was a fruity, caffeinated alcoholic drink that also contained taurine (an amino acid derivative contained is some foods and believed to have stimulant properties) and guarana (a South American caffeine-containing plant). The "Four" in Four Loko originally referred to the four primary ingredients: alcohol, caffeine, taurine, and guarana. Government agencies, alarmed by reports of the apparently dangerous effects of Four Loko, concluded that the problem resulted from the combination of alcohol with stimulants, especially caffeine. It was claimed that the stimulant masked the intoxicating effects of alcohol, encouraging excess alcohol consumption. The Food and Drug Administration (FDA) decided that caffeine was an illegal additive to an alcoholic beverage. As stated in a November 18, 2010, letter to several companies making such drinks (including Phusion Projects), the FDA said that consumption of caffeine-containing alcoholic beverages could lead to "hazardous and life-threatening situations."[9] The manufacturers were given 15 days to remove caffeine from their drinks, and they complied (removing taurine and guarana as well).

Prior to compelled decaffeination, Four Loko contained 12 percent alcohol (6 percent in some jurisdictions), and an undisclosed amount of caffeine. (According to the manufacturer, the caffeine content was comparable to that found in a cup of coffee). Although caffeine is generally accepted as the villain in the Four Loko story, the evidence that the stimulant modulates either the physiological, objective behavioral, or subjectively rated effects of alcohol is far from clear. Different researchers have concluded that caffeine increases, decreases, and has no effect on the intoxicating effects of alcohol.[10] Based strictly on pharmacology, drinking a can of Four Loko (23.5 ounces) should have had about the same effect as a bottle of wine and some coffee. Even the cost of Four Loko is comparable to the wine and coffee (if you buy Trader Joe's "Four Buck Chuck"). Why did this particular beverage cause so many people to become so inebriated that they required hospitalization? An answer was intuited by the *New York Times* columnist Frank Bruni: "If you set out to engineer a booze delivery system that is as cloying, deceptive and divorced from the usual smells, tastes and presentation of alcohol as possible, you'd be hard pressed to come up with something more impressive than Four Loko."[11] Four Loko (and similar beverages) induce an exaggerated effect because they provide alcohol in an unusual context.

We may surmise that, for most undergraduates, Four Loko provides alcohol in a beverage with a very novel flavor. As noted by Bruni, Four Loko, a "biliously colored," sweet, synthetically fruity beverage, is an unusual medium for alcohol: "It's a malt liquor in confectionary drag." It is likely that the reported enhanced-intoxicating properties of this beverage are not simply a result of the use of a fruity flavor—rather it is the use of a confectionary-like fruity flavor (and color) that, prior to the arrival of Four Loko, has likely not been paired with alcohol. Bruni describes "watermelon" flavored Four Loko as follows:

> The watermelon-flavored Four Loko, for example, is a shade of rosy pink that puts me in mind of sherbet. Or bridesmaid dresses.
>
> Or maybe Bubble Yum bubblegum. In fact, the watermelon tasted somewhat like that too. It certainly didn't bear any relation to any melon that I've ever tripped across—or, for that matter, to any known fruit. Its sweetness is more generic and synthetic, and makes Hi-C seem like a blast of unsullied farm-to-table goodness.[12]

Examination of the Four Loko web site (fourloko.com) indicates that there are even more novel-flavored Four Loko beverages. The company still makes the watermelon Four Loko, but some of the flavors are new and unusual. A "Black"-flavored beverage has some ill-defined flavor ("We won't tell you what it tastes like—you just have to find out"), as does "Gold"-flavored Four Loko ("Tastes like Gold. Not much more we can say"), and "Warheads Sour Cosmic Punch" ("the next big bang in sour drinks"). The alcohol content in some of these new Four Loko beverages has been increased to 14 percent.

In summary, it is likely that many people have become very drunk after consuming Four Loko because the beverage provides a novel context for alcohol; alcohol tolerance, having been acquired in the context of certain flavor cues, may not be exhibited in the context of Four Loko flavor cues. The Four Loko drinker is like participants in one of the previously described experiments who display excessive intoxication after consuming alcohol in a beverage with a novel color and flavor (e.g., blue-colored and peppermint-flavored).

As we have already seen, heroin addicts lose their tolerance if they administer the drug in an unfamiliar situation—they are at risk for heroin overdose. Similarly, college undergraduates who consume alcohol in an unfamiliar situation (novel flavor) do not display the expected level of alcohol tolerance—rather they display heightened intoxication and risk alcohol overdose.

In addition to the many studies with humans of the conditioning analysis of alcohol tolerance, there are many studies with rats. Various predictions concerning the role of Pavlovian conditioning in alcohol tolerance have been confirmed in these rat studies, using various measures of alcohol's effects (depression in body temperature, difficulty in maintaining balance, depressed activity, and decreased sensitivity to a painful stimulus).[13] There is even a demonstration that honeybees become tolerant to alcohol, and that this tolerance is due to Pavlovian conditioning. The bees were repeatedly presented with alcohol vapor paired with a distinctive odor. Based on assessment of activity, the bees displayed situational specificity of tolerance and conditional compensatory responding. That is, they were tolerant to alcohol only when they received the drug in the presence of the distinctive odor, and they displayed hyperreactivity when they were exposed to the alcohol-paired odor but no alcohol was presented.[14]

Pavlovian conditioning also accounts for cross-tolerance between alcohol and other drugs. Rats made tolerant to the hypothermic effect (lowering of body temperature) of a barbiturate, pentobarbital, were also tolerant to the hypothermic effect of alcohol, but only if the alcohol test occurred in the same environment in which the pentobarbital was administered.[15] College students tolerant to the heart-rate elevating effect of nicotine in smoked cigarettes were tolerant to the heart-rate elevating effect of alcohol only if the alcohol was consumed in the same environment in which they smoked.[16]

9 Victimized by Pavlovian Conditioning

> On two separate occasions, psychiatrists at the Lexington hospital related that in group therapy with long detoxified addicts, the patients would suddenly blow their noses, wipe their eyes, and yawn incessantly when the subject under discussion turned to dope. The psychiatrists, unaware of the conditioning theory of relapse, were puzzled by the reappearance of opioid-abstinence phenomena three to six months after detoxification.
> —Abraham Wikler, *Opioid Dependence: Mechanisms and Treatment* (New York: Plenum, 1980), 180–181

Conditional responses, like those seen in the presence of stimuli that are paired with heroin (or alcohol, or caffeine, or any of a variety of other drugs) serve to protect the drug-taker. The benefit of mitigating an event that threatens survival, in a timely manner, is clear. It can be a lifesaver, but these anticipatory responses can sometimes have problematic effects. Consider, for example, that you are in the presence of drug-paired cues but no drug is administered. In anticipation of the drug you are automatically compelled to exhibit the appropriate learned response that usually serves to lessen the drug effect. Because the drug does not arrive you are left with an anticipatory drug response that achieves full expression because there is no drug effect to modify it.

We associate paired events subconsciously. We cannot will ourselves to avoid anticipating a second event, given that we are presented with the first, assuming that the two events have a history of being paired. As Dr. Benjamin Rush noted in 1805, the "operation of the human mind obliges it to associate ideas, accidentally or otherwise combined."[1] Pavlov's dog salivated in response to a tone that reliably signaled dry food, and this exhibition of a learned response occurred without any explicit understanding of a cause (tone) and effect (dryness in the mouth) relationship.

The automatic nature of association-by-pairing is illustrated by the occasional maladaptive nature of learned responses. Although conditional responses are crucial for our survival, we sometimes wish they didn't occur. Sometimes we are presented with the first of two events that had been paired in the past, display the conditional response that automatically occurs (and that would normally lessen the effect of the forthcoming event), but the second event, the unconditional stimulus, does not occur. We are left with a preparatory response, but there is nothing to prepare for.

Consider the "broken escalator phenomenon." We have had a lot of experience riding escalators in, for example, department stores, shopping centers, airports, subways, office buildings, and hotels. Occasionally, we encounter one that is not working. When we do, we must ascend or descend this broken escalator in the same manner as we use ordinary stairs. However, unlike our experience with stairs, most people experience unsteadiness or vertigo while negotiating the broken escalator—some even stumble. The broken escalator effect has been extensively investigated in the laboratory.[2] It is due to Pavlovian conditioning. We have learned to make postural adjustments when riding an escalator. When the escalator was a novelty, novice riders sometimes were flustered by the experience of the moving staircase. In 1898, one of the first escalators for public use was installed in Harrods department store in London. Early users of the escalator were discombobulated: "Customers unnerved by the experience were revived by shopmen dispensing free smelling salts and cognac."[3] Children, who do not have a lot of experience in riding escalators, are especially prone to falling and suffering injuries in their early attempts at using the escalator.[4]

Experienced escalator riders have learned (without any conscious awareness) the trick of not falling while the ground moves under them at an angle. In the presence of escalator-paired stimuli (the sight of the escalator, grasping the handrail, and so on), we make many postural and gait adjustments to keep us upright and maintain our dignity. This works very well when we are in the presence of escalator-paired stimuli and the escalator is functional. However, our escalator-anticipatory responses do not serve us well when the escalator isn't working. When we are confronted with the broken escalator, even when we know that the machine is not working and there is no need to prepare for a moving-escalator-induced threat to our balance, we nevertheless make escalator-anticipatory responses when we ascend or descend the nonfunctional escalator. These unwanted and unneeded adjustments now have a counterproductive effect. Since there is no actual ground movement to cancel these postural corrections, they cause us to wobble a bit. This is just one example of how we are compelled to make the conditional response in the presence of the conditional stimulus, even when we know that it is unnecessary, or even maladaptive. Pavlovian conditioning has victimized us.

A film distributed in 1934 amusingly depicted the inevitability of the conditional response occurring in the presence of the conditional stimulus. For about two decades, beginning in the 1920s, Hal Roach studios produced a popular series of short films featuring "The Little Rascals"—child actors portraying a motley collection of poor and mischievous ragamuffins. In one of these films, *Mike Fright*, the Rascals enter an audition for a children's musical radio show.[5] They sabotage the audition of a competitor, the snobby "Little Leonard." With the help of Pavlovian conditioning Leonard's initially competent rendition of "Wild Irish Rose" on the trumpet deteriorates into discordant noise when some of the Rascals in the audience try to interfere with his trumpet playing by sucking on lemon slices. When Leonard sees these Rascals he can no longer play the trumpet because he automatically starts to salivate profusely. Leonard's response was involuntary and unwanted. His plight provides another illustration of the inevitability of the conditional response when the conditional stimulus is presented.

It's easy to understand why a lemon is a good conditional stimulus for salivation. A bit of lemon juice in your mouth unconditionally elicits salivation as a reflex response. This salivation adaptively dilutes the citric acid and prevents irritation of the sensitive oral mucosa. Lemon juice in the mouth is signaled by several conditional stimuli, such as the sight and smell of the lemon. We cannot will ourselves to *not* salivate when we suck on a lemon. Similarly, we cannot will ourselves to not salivate when we are confronted with lemon-associated stimuli. Results of laboratory studies (conducted many years after the release of *Mike Fright*) demonstrated that subjects salivate when they handle lemons or view an experimenter cutting a lemon, even if they are explicitly told that they will not consume the fruit.[6] Little Leonard was a victim of Pavlovian conditioning.

Drug addicts (and former addicts) also can be victims of Pavlovian conditioning. Consider the situation in which the long-abstinent former addict is in an environment where he or she had frequently used drugs in the past, or it is the time of day when the drug typically was administered, or any other of a variety of drug-associated stimuli are present. The individual inevitably displays the conditional responses that previously would have been adaptive. Such responses decrease the drug effect previously encountered in the presence of these stimuli and could save the addict's life (if the drug usually encountered in these circumstances was administered). However, if the anticipated drug is not forthcoming, the learned drug-preparatory responses achieve full expression because they are not countered by any drug effect. The conditional responses exhibited in such circumstances typically are not recognized or labeled as drug-anticipatory learned responses. Rather, they are (mis-)labeled drug "withdrawal symptoms." Such responses have also been studied in rats. Rats that display tolerance to morphine when the drug is administered in the usual morphine administration environment display "withdrawal symptoms" in the morphine administration environment when not administered the usual morphine.[7]

Two defining characteristics of addiction are drug tolerance and drug withdrawal symptoms. The correlation between tolerance (when the drug is administered) and the appearance of withdrawal symptoms (when the drug is not administered) has been observed for a very long time. As noted by addiction researchers Constantine Poulos and Harold Cappell, "the fact that a strong relationship exists between the degree of tolerance and the intensity of withdrawal must be taken into consideration in evaluating the kind of basic mechanism involved." These investigators went on to point out that, in addition to tolerance and withdrawal symptoms being highly correlated, withdrawal symptoms are compensatory homeostatic responses: "As a general pharmacological principle, it can be asserted that withdrawal effects are usually opposite to acute drug effects."[8] The relationship between tolerance and withdrawal, and the fact that most withdrawal symptoms are drug-compensatory homeostatic responses, are attributable to the fact they are both manifestations of the same conditional drug response: "It is the anticipation of the drug, rather than the drug itself, that is responsible for these [withdrawal] symptoms ... some drug 'withdrawal symptoms' are, more accurately, drug 'preparation symptoms.'"[9] These symptoms are not due to the cumulative baneful effects of the prior drug administrations, but rather to the preparation for the next drug administration. These drug-preparation symptoms are the ghosts that haunt the addict.

In discussing the role of conditional responses in so-called withdrawal symptoms, it is important to make a distinction between the acute withdrawal reactions seen shortly after the initiation of abstinence, and the so-called withdrawal symptoms seen long after the last drug administration (chronic withdrawal). Acute withdrawal symptoms are due to the slowly decaying homeostatic response unconditionally elicited by the drug. If the individual has taken the drug many times, the acute withdrawal will be especially pronounced because there is a large conditional homeostatic response supplementing the drug-induced unconditional homeostatic response. Acute withdrawal symptoms may be uncomfortable, but they typically last only for days or, at most, a week. The intractability of drug addiction is not due to this immediate-post abstinence withdrawal period. Rather, the problem is relapse following completion of the acute withdrawal period—often long after the so-called "detoxification" period. Although detoxified addicts no longer experience unconditional homeostatic drug-compensatory responses (because they are not taking the drug), they still display conditional homeostatic drug-compensatory responses. Just as Little Leonard (who may not have eaten a lemon for a long time prior to his audition) is compelled to make a citric-acid preparatory response (i.e., salivate) in the presence of lemon-associated stimuli, the drug-experienced individual is compelled to make drug-preparatory responses in the presence of drug-associated stimuli. These drug-preparatory responses are the ghost of prior drug use—the ghost that haunts the addict. Although such chronic symptoms are really a manifestation of drug preparation, rather than drug withdrawal, we will stick with generally accepted terminology and refer to them as "withdrawal symptoms" rather than "preparation symptoms."

There are many laboratory experiments confirming the observations that Benjamin Rush made in the early 1800s concerning the powerful evocative effects of drug-paired stimuli. These experiments evaluated drug-dependent individuals and demonstrated that drug-associated stimuli are powerful elicitors of withdrawal symptoms. Former heroin addicts display physiological signs of narcotic withdrawal when they perform the "cooking up" ritual while being monitored by a polygraph, or when presented with a picture containing drug-related cues. Alcoholics and cigarette smokers similarly respond to the appropriate drug-associated cues with withdrawal symptoms and craving.[10] Coffee drinkers exhibit coffee withdrawal signs and crave the beverage when they are presented with pictures related to coffee drinking (e.g., coffee being poured into a cup).[11]

Similar findings have been obtained in experiments with animals. Joseph Ternes evaluated opioid effects in monkeys. He described the behavior of monkeys that were repeatedly injected with morphine while tape-recorded music played in the background (presumably for the entertainment of the experimenter). Following their participation in the research, when the monkeys were weaned from the drug and abstinent for several months, replaying the music caused the monkeys to display morphine withdrawal symptoms.[12] Rats with a history of drug administration display more behavioral withdrawal symptoms in a drug-paired environment than in an alternative environment.[13] Results of a recent study indicate that drug-paired cues elicit withdrawal symptoms, even in crayfish.[14]

Complementing the laboratory research are many case reports. Addicts, and clinicians who treat addicts, have observed that detoxified addicts, who no longer display withdrawal symptoms in the detoxification environment, do so when they return to an environment rich in drug-associated stimuli. The contribution of these stimuli to addiction has been noted even in long-detoxified former addicts. For example, addicts convicted and jailed may be abstinent for the duration of their sentence. Following an initial period of acute withdrawal distress early in their jailing they may find that they no longer experience withdrawal sickness and conclude that they are no longer addicted. However, following completion of their sentence (served in an environment devoid of cues that had been associated with drug use) they find that they again experience withdrawal symptoms when they return to an environment rich in drug-associated cues. This scenario has been noted by several addiction researchers. For example, addiction scientist Charles O'Brien described a narcotic addict in Philadelphia who was imprisoned and drug-free for six months: "He gained weight, felt like a new man, and decided that he was finished with drugs." However, when he was released from prison, "as the subway approached his stop he began sweating, tearing from his eyes, and gagging . . . as he got off the subway, he vomited on to the tracks. He soon bought drugs and was relieved."[15] Similarly, Benjamin Kissin studied New York City heroin addicts who were confined to Sing Sing, the federal penitentiary in Ossining, New York (about 40 miles from New York City): "Heroin addicts returning from Ossining to New York by train, after 5 years of incarceration and abstinence, experience acute withdrawal symptomatology as the train passes their old neighborhoods."[16]

When cigarette smokers are hospitalized they typically are prohibited from smoking by hospital policy. The hospital environment is very different from the patient's home environment, and the enforced cigarette abstinence often is not a tremendous hardship because the patients are not exposed to the usual smoking cues. Hospitalized smokers will often feel they are cured of their addiction to nicotine. However, in the very first day following discharge, when they return to an environment rich in smoking-paired cues, about a quarter of them return to smoking.[17]

There are many reports of patients who display withdrawal symptoms and crave drugs when confronted with cues that had signaled the drug in the past—for example, seeing the paraphernalia of addiction such as a syringe and tourniquet,[18] seeing slides depicting drug administration,[19] discussing drugs with others,[20] or even seeing actors seeming to inject heroin in a movie.[21] Is there conscious recognition that these recurring symptoms are really learned responses? Sociologist Patrick

Biernacki interviewed heroin addicts about the circumstances of their relapse. Some perspicacious addicts do realize that the ghost that haunts them is summoned by drug-paired stimuli, and that their chronic withdrawal distress results from learned associations. According to Biernacki, "one respondent likened himself to one of Pavlov's dogs when he felt the nausea accompanying a craving. He explained: 'I had the objectivity to even see my own behavior for what it was and that was like getting nauseous whenever I'd even think about fixing. Like one of Pavlov's dogs.'"[22] However, most addicts, and most people who treat addicts, do not realize that withdrawal symptoms are called forth by stimuli that had been paired with drug use. For example, some heroin addicts inexplicably experience withdrawal symptoms when confronted by the smells in a public toilet. Although these addicts have often injected themselves in the toilet, they do not make the connection between the odiferous stimulus and the drug.[23] Similarly, some addicts report that they feel withdrawal distress when they detect the sulfurous smell of a match that is recently extinguished by a nearby cigarette smoker. The addict does not recognize that this distinctive odor had previously been paired with the effects of heroin (the heroin-water mixture having been heated in a spoon with a match before it was drawn into a syringe and injected).[24]

A case of relapse in a former drug user, 14 months after successful detoxification, illustrates the potent role of drug-associated cues in relapse (even though the role of these cues is unknown to the addict):

> Harry turns into the bridge that will take him back over to the old neighborhood. It feels good to be free again, and he hasn't used any heroin since he left the street for a 14-month stint in jail. No debts, no habit (the jail detox was harsh but is now long past), no problems. But as his wheels hit the rough surface of the

bridge, his bowels begin to growl. As the skyline comes closer, he begins to yawn and his eyes water. He breaks out in sweat, gripping the wheel and trying to ignore the raw, acid taste in the back of his throat. He feels mounting panic, immediately recognizing this mouth-watery, nauseated feeling as the old sickness he left behind more than a year before. But here it is again. It can't be, but somehow it is. Muttering under his breath, Harry turns toward a familiar alley. He knows how to get rid of this kind of sickness, and fast.[25]

Whether or not the individual recognizes that his symptoms are conditional responses, he or she is compelled to exhibit them when confronted by the appropriate conditional stimuli. The drug addict (even the long-abstinent former addict) can no sooner inhibit the display of preparation/withdrawal symptoms than we can inhibit our conditional balance adjustments when we negotiate a broken escalator, or Little Leonard could inhibit the conditional salivary response that sabotaged his musical audition. These withdrawal symptoms are a basic homeostatic mechanism—they are the price paid for the beneficial effects of chronic drug tolerance.

Some homeostatic conditional responses, if not followed by the usual unconditional stimulus, are very uncomfortable. That's especially true of conditional responses made in preparation for some psychoactive drugs. The drugs ravage our physiology and elicit homeostatic responses that necessarily are distressing if they are elicited in the absence of the drug, and thus achieve full expression. For example, the physician and scientist Abraham Wikler (who was among the first to recognize the contribution of Pavlovian conditioning to drug addiction) described the case report of an addict who was oblivious to the role of drug-associated stimuli in relapse:

> After being detoxified and having served their sentence at the U.S. Public Health Service Hospital, the postaddict felt fine and had no craving for heroin or morphine but just before his release, or on

his way home, or after arriving in his drug-ridden environment, he felt sick, craved a fix, and then hustled to obtain it. Some postaddicts described the sickness in more detail: running nose, watery eyes, sweating, chills, nausea and vomiting—"like the flu, doc." One postaddict, a physician, remarked that the sickness resembled heroin abstinence phenomena, but he dismissed that interpretation as preposterous.[26]

Despite the physician/postaddict's skepticism, Wikler deduced that the flu-like symptoms seen in the presence of drug-paired stimuli were, in fact, opiate-compensatory learned responses. The "running nose, watering eyes" are opposite in direction to the secretory drying effects of the opiates. The "sweating," resulting from elevation in body temperature, is opposite to the drug-induced decrease in body temperature. The "chills" result from peripheral vasoconstriction (a decrease in diameter of the blood vessels near the surface of the skin), opposite to the peripheral vasodilatory effect of the opiates. The "nausea and vomiting" result from increased peristaltic activity (wave-like contractions of the alimentary canal), opposite to the opiate-induced decrease in peristaltic activity. If the usual drug were administered in the presence of these drug-associated stimuli, the effect of the drug would be adaptively minimized by these anticipatory homeostatic responses. Since there's no drug, they are withdrawal symptoms. The postaddict finds them distressing, and they are relieved only by using the drug again.

Well before there was appreciation of the role of Pavlovian conditioning in drug addiction, some observers of addiction (especially alcoholism) noted the importance of drug-associated stimuli. In 1835 Scottish physician Robert Macnish, in agreement with Benjamin Rush's earlier observations, noted the main problem in treating the alcoholic is achieving long-term

Victimized by Pavlovian Conditioning

abstinence: "To remove the habit of drunkenness from any one in whom it has been long established, is a task of peculiar difficulty. We not only have to contend against the cravings of the body, but against those of the mind."[27] Although Macnish wrote this 14 years before Pavlov was born, it was clear to Macnish that these "cravings of the mind" were provoked by stimuli that had been paired with alcohol. He noted:

> Man is very much the creature of habit. By drinking regularly at certain times, he feels the longing for liquor at the stated return of these periods—as after dinner, or immediately before going to bed, or whatever the period may be. He even feels it in certain companies, or in a particular tavern at which he is in the habit of taking his libations.[28]

Like Benjamin Rush, Robert Macnish suggested that the alcoholic could be cured by not exposing himself or herself to alcohol paired stimuli. He offered a simple treatment for the alcoholic. Move away from these alcohol-paired stimuli: "Let him, if he can manage it, remove from the place of his usual residence, and go somewhere else."[29] Can you, as Macnish suggested in 1835, lessen drug withdrawal distress simply by moving from an environment that is rich is drug-associated stimuli to somewhere else? Surprisingly, generations of researchers have, without acknowledging Robert Macnish, or Benjamin Rush, or Pavlovian conditioning, repeatedly rediscovered the efficacy of this "geographic cure."

10 The Geographic Cure

> In our observation, treatment staff commonly discourage relocation, on the assumption that the problem exists primarily within the person. Although opioid drug dependence does exist as a disorder within the person, the condition is modulated by the environment. We found that a relatively high percentage (31%) of treatment interaction combined with residence relocation led to one year or more of abstinence. This finding suggests that treatment staff should be mindful that relocation in some instances should be encouraged rather than discouraged.
> —James F. Maddux and David P. Desmond, "Residence Relocation Inhibits Opioid Dependence," *Archives of General Psychiatry* 39 (1982): 1317

The treatment of addiction does not represent a triumph of modern medicine. Many people who enter drug treatment programs do not complete the course of treatment. The overwhelming majority of those who do complete treatment subsequently relapse. Is there, as Robert Macnish suggested, an easy way to stop using drugs? Should the drug user who wants to quit simply, to paraphrase the real estate mantra, "relocate, relocate, relocate"? Since addiction results from the association of drug-paired cues with the drug effect, relocation to a new environment that is not filled with drug-paired cues should decrease the likelihood that the ghost of addiction will appear. Advocates of traditional drug treatment programs, such as Alcoholics Anonymous, are skeptical about geographic relocation as a treatment strategy:[1] "No matter where you go, there you are"—"There you are" with (depending on your view of addiction) the same addictive personality, or errant DNA, or neurochemical abnormalities, or neuroanatomical defects, or genetic predisposition to addiction. However, contrary to the dogma of Alcoholics Anonymous, but in agreement with the conditioning interpretation of addiction, there is evidence that relocation often works. When you go to a new environment, "there you are" indeed, but (with any luck) your old drug-associated stimuli will not be there.

In most evaluations of the geographic cure, former addicts are questioned about the circumstances surrounding their cessation of drug use, or the incidence of abstinence is compared in addicts who chose to move to those who did not move. An early attempt to evaluate the effectiveness of relocation as a cure for addiction was reported in 1966 by sociologist Robert Schasre. He located 22 former addicts in Los Angeles who had been abstinent for 8 to 16 years. Schasre stated that he was especially interested in this group because none of these 22 ever made an explicit decision to attempt to stop using drugs; rather, they just stopped. For 13 of these respondents, the explanation for their termination of drug use was simple: their supplier was no longer available. For the remaining 9 cases, geographic relocation immediately preceded abstinence: "In seven of these nine cases, where the ex-user's family had moved either from the neighborhood or out of town, it was reported they just 'lost interest' in using. None of these individuals, six of whom remained in the Los Angeles area, and one of whom moved to Lompoc, California, recounted any efforts to procure narcotics after they had moved from the area where they had used."[2]

In 1969, another researcher reported the results of his interviews with 109 former heroin addicts in Detroit. Physical relocation was significantly associated with abstinence from illicit drugs: "It appears that for a large group of a treatment population (almost 40%) cessation of illegal drug use meant moving away physically from an area of high drug use."[3] Ten years later a similar finding was reported in Sweden: "When asked what they had done to change their lives in order to give up drugs, a majority of the respondents answered that they had felt it necessary to change residence."[4]

In August 2005 Hurricane Katrina damaged most of the housing stock in New Orleans. There was a widespread diversion of New Orleans parolees (including those with a history of drug abuse) to other residential locations in Louisiana. Reincarceration of the parolees with a history of drug abuse one year later was evaluated. Parolees who returned to their original New Orleans environment were more likely to be reincarcerated than parolees who remained in the new environment. The authors concluded "relocation is consequential because it separates individuals from . . . environmental cues associated with prior drug use."[5]

A study conducted in Sydney, Australia, evaluated willpower in drug users who recovered from addiction. Willpower was important, but not as important as residence relocation:

> When cravings and temptations are not experienced, people need not rely on willpower. A major reason for this absence of cravings and temptations is that participants in recovery remove themselves from the environment in which they used to use and avoid friends from their using days. . . . Conversely, participants

who have not been successful in controlling use often report that they know that they should avoid old environments, but face very significant financial or social obstacles to moving to a new environment.[6]

Other findings attesting to the beneficial effect of residence relocation were obtained in studies conducted in Vancouver,[7] Baltimore,[8] Atlanta,[9] Canberra,[10] and San Antonio.[11] The San Antonio results were especially compelling: The frequency of one-year abstinence was three times higher in relocated respondents than in respondents staying in San Antonio. Eighty-one percent of the relocated abstinent patients who returned to San Antonio relapsed within one month.

In summary, evaluation of the experiences of drug addicts suggests that residence relocation is a good prescription for stopping drug use. In addition to these reports, there has been a monumental epidemiological study, conducted in response to a perceived national crisis, attesting to the beneficial effects of residential relocation in terminating drug abuse. The study involved heroin use by returning Vietnam veterans.

Disaffected youth in the 1960s presented many challenges to the government. Among them was drug abuse. In a July 1969 "Special Message to the Congress on Control of Narcotics and Dangerous Drugs," President Richard Nixon noted that "the number of narcotics addicts across the United States is now estimated to be in the hundreds of thousands," and made the case for new funding and legislation to deal with the problem.[12] The funding was granted and the legislation was passed, but this proclamation of the "war on drugs" had little impact on the problem. The most comprehensive treatment programs at the time involved protracted residency/incarceration in one of the Federal Medical Centers in Fort Worth, Texas, or Lexington, Kentucky. These closely supervised interventions in an isolated drug-free environment resulted, of course, in abstinence. No drugs were available to these patients. However, following release, 90 percent of the alumni of these programs relapsed to drug use: "Such pessimistic outcomes understandably lead to the widespread belief that opiate addiction was intractable and even experimental use of this illicit drug was like playing Russian roulette with one bullet chamber empty."[13]

The government of the Vietnam era also faced increasing pressure resulting from a succession of rallies protesting the war in Vietnam. The twin concerns of drug abuse and Vietnam protests came together in scattered reports of heroin use by U.S. soldiers stationed in Vietnam. The drug was very cheap and widely available.

Two congressmen, Robert Steele (R-CT) and Morgan Murphy (D-IL), visited Vietnam in the spring of 1971 to investigate the reports. On April 29 they presented an alarming message to the White House. By their estimate, 10 to 20 percent of the soldiers in Vietnam were heroin addicts. Steele told a *New York Times* reporter, "the soldier going to South Vietnam today runs a far greater risk of becoming a heroin addict than a combat casualty."[14] From the perspective of the government, and especially the Nixon presidency, this military heroin use undermined the war effort. It also augured a grave domestic problem. The United States was withdrawing up to 1,000 soldiers a day from Vietnam. When they were discharged, there would be an alarming increase in the heroin addict population in the United States. Moreover, these newly arriving addicts would be trained fighters: "The specter of weapons-trained, addicted combat veterans joining the deadly struggle for drugs [in the streets of America] is ominous," according to an article that appeared in *Time* magazine.[15]

The nation's overcrowded and ineffective drug-treatment facilities were manifestly unsuccessful in dealing with the existing domestic problem. How would they handle the flood of new addicts? Something had to be done, and done quickly. Moreover, any strategy to deal with the crisis had to be implemented with some finesse. Any alarming message about an impending surge in the American heroin addict population attributable to returning Vietnam veterans would provide further ammunition to those protesting this very unpopular war.

The Vietnam addiction problem combined several matters of great concern to citizens. According to a Gallup poll, conducted and released in June 1971, Americans thought that the three biggest problems facing their country were the Vietnam War, the financial situation, and drug problems.[16] To address the Vietnam addiction crisis President Richard Nixon needed money and new powers, touching all the bases highlighted in the Gallup poll. Nixon realized it would be imprudent to justify the new tools needed to fight addiction by candidly describing what his advisors claimed was a likely scenario—massive domestic strife stemming from a huge influx of addicts as a result of U.S. involvement in Vietnam. Since there is a very high relapse rate following all known forms of treatment, it was expected that a new, large population of relapsing heroin addicts would substantially add to the civilian addict population. This led to serious concerns in the Senate. According to Senate testimony, "this will obviously lead to crime and other problems with law enforcement when he (the returning Vietnam heroin user) brings his addiction home. . . . They will be unable to cut off this drug use."[17]

On June 17, 1971, President Nixon presented another special message to Congress, "Drug Abuse Prevention and Control." In asking Congress for extraordinary powers, and an additional

155 million dollars, Nixon did not emphasize an impending emergency resulting from returning heroin-addicted veterans. Rather, he highlighted the effects of drug use on domestic criminal activity and public health:

> Despite the fact that drug addiction destroys lives, destroys families, and destroys communities, we are still not moving fast enough to meet the problem in an effective way. Our efforts are strained through the Federal bureaucracy. Of those we can reach at all under the present Federal system—and the number is relatively small—of those we try to help and who want help, we cure only a tragically small percentage. . . . The magnitude of the problem, the national and international implications of the problem, and the limited capacities of States and cities to deal with the problem all reinforce the conclusion that coordination of this effort must take place at the highest levels of the Federal Government. Therefore, I propose the establishment of a central authority with overall responsibility for all major Federal drug abuse prevention, education, treatment, rehabilitation, training, and research programs in all Federal agencies. This authority would be known as the Special Action Office of Drug Abuse Prevention. It would be located within the Executive Office of the President and would be headed by a Director accountable to the President.[18]

In his congressional message Nixon did mention the Vietnam drug problem but minimized its severity: Vietnam drug use was "disheartening," but "by no means a major part of the American narcotics problem." Without stressing the magnitude of the impending emergency predicted by Representatives Steele and Murphy, Nixon was assembling machinery to deal with it. Because of a fortunate selection of the person to be the inaugural Director of the Special Action Office of Drug Abuse Prevention, the stage was set for an extraordinary epidemiological study of residence relocation and drug addiction.

White House aides settled on Jerome Jaffe as the most qualified person to head the new agency. Jaffe was a 37-year-old psychiatrist, on the faculty of the University of Chicago, with extensive experience in the treatment of drug addiction. He became the first "Drug Czar" (although that unofficial title wasn't in general use until about ten years later). At the time of Jaffe's appointment, the military's response to heroin use was punitive. Identified users were subject to dishonorable discharge, court-martial, and imprisonment.

Jaffe's background did not include politics or the military. He was a scientist and a clinician with extensive experience in treating heroin addiction. He advocated a public-health, rather than punitive, approach to addiction. As a scientist, he was committed to evaluating the effect of intervention strategies. He insisted that all soldiers about to leave Vietnam have urine tests that could detect opiate metabolites. Those found to be users would be detoxified for five to seven days prior to their return to the United States. They then would, if necessary, receive further treatment when they returned to the States. The returning soldiers knew that they would be tested immediately prior to their scheduled departure, and only had to be abstinent for about three days prior to the test for the test results to be negative. Jaffe thought that the threat of a delayed departure would motivate the very occasional users of heroin to refrain from using the drug prior to their scheduled departure, and thus not test positive. Only true, intransigent addicts would be unable to refrain from heroin use immediately prior to the test. The prevalence of hard-core addiction could be estimated from the results of the mandatory urine analysis. Those testing positive would not be subject to any punishment, other than the delayed departure from Vietnam due to detoxification.

Jaffe's plan met considerable resistance from the military when he briefed them on May 30, 1971. The generals and admirals were not enthusiastic about treating addicts with kid gloves. In addition, they noted that the complicated logistics of bringing so many troops home each day was formidable and claimed that requiring each to provide a urine specimen right before the scheduled departure would hopelessly complicate the task. Jaffe's reply to the assembled high-ranking officers was blunt: "I cannot believe that the mightiest army on earth can't get its troops to piss in a bottle."[19] Jaffe prevailed. In Jaffe's own words:

> I also pointed out that implementing this plan would require changing the Code of Military Justice as it related to drugs. It seemed to me that requiring the men to provide urine specimens when there was a risk that doing so could lead to criminal punishment violated their Constitutional rights. While I recognized that persuading the military to forgo punitive consequences for heroin use would be difficult, I was reasonably sure that a certain and immediate small adverse consequence (a delay in returning home) would have a greater effect on deterring heroin use, even for those who were addicted, than the far less certain and more remote possibility of a greater adverse consequence (bad conduct or dishonorable discharge).[20]

Jaffe's plan was instituted in July 1971. Just before boarding the waiting aircraft to leave Vietnam, each soldier had to provide a urine sample. The samples were analyzed within 30 seconds, and those testing positive were immediately taken to a detoxification area, where they were forced to go cold turkey for a week. The Secretary of Defense, Melvin Laird, decreed that a positive urine test did not have any disciplinary consequences: "With a stroke of the pen, the Nixon administration had effectively decriminalized drug use within the military."[21]

Jaffe realized that his program would generate a unique data set. He sought someone with the background and skills to evaluate the Vietnam heroin addiction findings and approached

Professor Lee Robins in July 1971. Robins was a sociologist by training, and a professor in the Psychiatry Department at Washington University in St. Louis. It was a wonderful choice, and Robins agreed to take on the task. This research, by Robins and her collaborators, stands as a superlative demonstration of the power of epidemiological research. It provides the most compelling data we have concerning the effect of residence relocation on cessation of drug use.

At Robins's request, the Department of Defense provided her team with information about all Vietnam returnees for the month of September 1971 (chosen because that was the first month in which Jaffe's urine screening and detoxification program was in full operation). From this population, about 900 were randomly selected for follow-up interviews between May and October 1972 (8 to 12 months after their return from Vietnam). Approximately half of this sample were randomly selected among all men leaving Vietnam in the selected month, and the other half were randomly selected among those that tested positive for heroin at the departure screening. (There was some overlap between the two samples.) Urine specimens were collected from almost all the interviewees. Additionally, a random sample of about two-thirds of the original participants was re-interviewed in 1974, approximately three years after their return from Vietnam. Robins's data indicated that about 20 percent of the soldiers in Vietnam were (by most definitions) addicted to heroin while serving their tours. Robins grasped the magnitude of the problem: "If heroin addiction among these [returning] soldiers was as chronic and unresponsive to treatment as it had been found to be in the heroin addicts seen in the U.S. Hospitals in Lexington and Ft. Worth, there was reason for concern."[22]

Fortunately, the potential public health disaster did not materialize. Unlike most civilian addicts, who were treated and returned to their usual environment, these Vietnam addicts returned to an environment very different from that in which they used drugs. They also evidenced much less relapse than civilian addicts. In one report, narcotic use in the United States by returned veterans addicted in Vietnam was compared to that seen in addicts of comparable age treated at the large Federal facilities in Lexington and Fort Worth.[23] Those addicted in Vietnam (and returned to a very different environment) were considerably less likely to relapse than those addicted in the environment to which they subsequently returned. Indeed, the veterans evidenced "rates of remission unheard of among narcotics addicts treated in the United States."[24] Many of Robins's conclusions have been substantially confirmed in a more recent follow up study of a different population of returned soldiers who were addicted in Vietnam.[25]

According to Robins, the low rate of relapse in Vietnam veterans was unexpected: "The surprisingly low levels of readdiction . . . are findings still not entirely incorporated into public and scientific views of heroin addiction."[26] In fact, the Vietnam addiction data should not have been unexpected. Recall that way back in 1835 Robert Macnish proposed that residence relocation cures addiction, and there have been many studies (prior to evaluations of readdiction of returning Vietnam veterans) confirming Macnish's suggestion. The Vietnam addiction experience is consistent with "scientific views of heroin addiction," which attribute relapse to a conditional homeostatic response elicited by the usual drug administration cues.

There are, understandably, no experimental studies of the efficacy of the geographic cure for human addicts; addicts cannot be randomly assigned to either stay in their usual environment or to relocate. By necessity, then, studies of the geographic cure are correlational. Although such results are consistent with a view of addiction that emphasizes the importance of drug-associated stimuli, there are other interpretations. Perhaps addicts who are motivated to give up their addiction are especially prone to "starting over" by relocating to a new environment. It is possible that, compared to the old environment, the new environment is one with less access to drugs, or one with more stringent policing. Perhaps a new environment provides novel distractions so that the relocated addict finds other, nonpharmacological diversions. Perhaps soldiers in Vietnam turned to heroin use to alleviate the stresses of being in a war zone—stresses that were eliminated when they left.

The experimental analysis of relocation and relapse can be done in experiments only with nonhumans. In such experiments we can evaluate relapse after randomly assigning addicted animals to environments that are, or are not, rich in the usual drug-associated stimuli (and do not differ with respect to potentially confounding variables). Such experiments have been done.

In one such study, rats were addicted to morphine by having morphine-adulterated water as their only drinking solution for 60 days. They were then withdrawn from morphine for 30 days. Following this 30-day abstinence period, the detoxified rats were again given the opportunity to drink the morphine solution. For half the rats, this relapse assessment occurred in the same environment as that used during the addiction phase. For the remaining rats, this final phase of the experiment took place in a very different environment. Relapse was greater in those rats offered the morphine solution in the environment

The Geographic Cure

where original addiction had occurred than when relapse assessment occurred in an alternative environment.[27] That is, the geographic cure worked for these rats.

Similar results were obtained in another experiment in which rats had experience with two distinctively different environments. In one of the two environments they were injected with morphine, and in the other with physiologically inert saline. This procedure ensured that the animals were equally familiar with both environments. The rats subsequently were given the opportunity to drink a morphine solution in both environments. They voluntarily drugged themselves with morphine more when the opiate solution was offered in the morphine-paired environment than when it was offered in the saline-paired environment.[28] Again, removal from drug-paired environmental cues decreased drug use in rats.

These results of experiments with drug-addicted rodents confirm reports of the experiences of human drug addicts. Following detoxification, removal of the addict from the addiction environment is a good prescription for stopping drug use. For both humans and nonhuman animals, placement in an environment that is not filled with drug-associated stimuli reduces the likelihood that they will experience the conditional responses that are withdrawal symptoms. They are not confronted by the ghost that haunts the addict.

11 Expected and Unexpected Drugs

> There is increasing evidence that the effects of a variety of drugs are different if they are self-administered rather than passively received.
> —James MacRae and Shepard Siegel, "The Role of Self-administration in Morphine Withdrawal in Rats," *Psychobiology* 25 (1997): 77

Stimuli that have been paired with drug administration produce conditional responses whether or not the drug is administered. These conditional responses decrease the effect of the drug when the drug is taken and are expressed as so-called withdrawal symptoms when the drug is not taken. Such drug-paired stimuli, including the environment in which heroin is habitually administered, raise an expectation that a drug effect is imminent. In other words, an expected drug has a smaller effect than an unexpected drug, and if an expected drug is not administered withdrawal symptoms appear.

There are ways to evaluate the effects of drug-expectation on drug effects that do not involve explicit manipulation of external environmental cues. One way to administer a drug unexpectedly is to, unpredictably, compel consumption. Consider this far-fetched scenario: You are confined in some isolated environment and, every once in a while, a mad scientist unexpectedly thrusts a shot of liquor at you and orders you to drink it then and there. The alcohol consumed in this manner should be especially intoxicating. It is unexpected, and you do not have an opportunity to make anticipatory homeostatic responses that would lessen the effects of the alcohol.

Actually, this situation is not so far-fetched. The consequences of such compelled alcohol administration were described in an article published over half a century ago in the prestigious *Journal of Pharmacology and Experimental Therapeutics*. The extraordinary experiment was not conducted by a mad scientist, but rather by the well-established married researchers, Nancy Mello and Jack Mendelson. Both were at the National Center for the Prevention and Control of Alcoholism, part of the National Institute of Mental Health (Mendelson was Chief of the Center). The research, conducted in 1970, couldn't be conducted today. A research ethics board would have conniptions if presented with a research proposal that involved forcing alcoholics to consume alcohol.

The subjects for this Mello and Mendelson experiment were eight alcoholic males at an inpatient treatment facility. The men volunteered to participate in a study in which they would be provided with lots and lots of free bourbon. They were evaluated while consuming the drink in two conditions, each condition lasting 20 days. In the first condition, which the experimenters labeled "programmed alcohol administration," but might be better termed "coerced alcohol administration," the men were instructed to consume a proffered glass of bourbon six times per day: once every four hours around the clock (2 a.m., 6 a.m., 10 a.m., 2 p.m., 6 p.m., and 10 p.m.). Although the authors are not explicit on this point, presumably the men were often sleeping at the time scheduled for their drink, and they had to be awakened to keep to the rigid schedule. The volume of the drink was systematically escalated until each subject was given as much bourbon as they could handle until, by the last 14 days, the participants were offered between 26 and 32 ounces of bourbon per day ("unless gastritis or other intercurrent illness necessitated lowering the dosage"). After 20 days on this schedule, the men underwent a ten-day detoxification period, during which their alcohol withdrawal symptoms were tabulated. These eight men then entered the second, 20-day alcohol-drinking phase of the experiment. During this second "spontaneous drinking" or "free choice" phase, each man was provided with 33 tokens per day. Each token could be exchanged for one ounce of bourbon. The men were free to use, or not use, as many of the 33 tokens each day as they wished, and there were no constraints as to how much alcohol they could "buy" with their tokens at any one time. This free-choice phase was also followed by another detoxification period during which withdrawal symptoms again were measured.

The free-choice bourbon, consumed during the second phase of the experiment, was totally expected. The subjects knew they were about to experience the effects of the drink because, before consuming it, they voluntarily exchanged their token for a shot. The stimulus that is paired with the self-administered drug is internal. The stimulus is experienced by the drug-taker, but not by an outside observer. In contrast with programmed alcohol consumption, subjects had extensive experience with free-choice alcohol consumption prior to entering the study. Although the programmed alcohol, consumed in the first phase of the experiment, was also somewhat predictable (it arrived every four hours), the subjects likely were not always attending to the time or might be sleeping when the bourbon was thrust upon them. They had less of an opportunity to anticipate the programmed drink than the voluntarily consumed drink.

Mello and Mendelson reported that all eight subjects in the experiment drank more alcohol when they self-administered the drug than when the experimenter administered the drug. In fact, during the first phase of the experiment, when the subjects were instructed to consume the proffered drink, five of the eight simply could not sustain ingestion of all the programmed amount of alcohol—it made them sick. They developed gastritis and were vomiting, and the amount of alcohol that they were given had to be decreased. However, during the spontaneous-drinking phase of the experiment, these same five men had no difficulty consuming much more than their previously intolerable programmed maximum dosage, and none had any discernable gastrointestinal problems. Not only did all participants in the experiment drink more alcohol when they self-administered the drug than when the experimenter administered the drug, but they also had much higher blood alcohol levels. Thus, based on blood alcohol levels, the spontaneously consumed alcohol should be more intoxicating than the programmed alcohol, but the opposite was found. When the subjects knew they were getting the drug, because they chose to self-administer it, they were better able to compensate for the intoxicating effects. The authors were surprised by "the unexpected finding that subjects were able to tolerate large quantities of alcohol under free choice conditions better than smaller doses of alcohol administered on a programmed basis."[1]

When a drug is self-administered, it is expected, just as surely as the drug is expected when it is administered in the presence of drug-associated environmental stimuli. Mello and Mendelson were surprised by their finding that self-administered alcohol was better tolerated than experimenter-administered because, at the time they did their research, there was little appreciation of the role of drug anticipation in drug tolerance. Based on evidence obtained after the Mello and Mendelson experiment, we should not be surprised by these results. The greater tolerance observed when the alcohol was expected (self-administered) than when it was unexpected (compelled consumption) was due to the relatively greater conditional homeostatic responses that occur when the drug can be anticipated.

Similar results were subsequently reported by drug researchers Chris-Ellyn Johanson and Charles Schuster. They studied the effects of phencyclidine ("angel dust," an animal anesthetic sometimes abused by humans) in monkeys. Tolerance was greater in monkeys that self-administered rather than passively received the drug. In fact, passive receipt of phencyclidine frequently was lethal "at dose levels at or below those self-administered, which animals survived."[2]

When we decide that we will self-administer a drug, we have internal stimuli—neurological events that urge us to drink the alcohol (or inject heroin or smoke a cigarette). These internal stimuli (termed "self-administration cues") are absent when we are obliged to take a drug that is unpredictably presented to us. Self-administration cues have been termed "private cues." Unlike external, environmental cues, self-administration cues (until they impel action) are apparent only to the drug-taker, and not to an observer. Such private cues function like environmental cues in decreasing the effects of predictable drugs.

Conditional homeostatic responses not only contribute to tolerance but also to withdrawal symptoms. Mello and Mendelson evaluated the severity of withdrawal symptoms during the drying out periods that followed each phase of the experiment. When the drug no longer is available, and these drug anticipatory responses achieve full expression, they should be greater following a history of expected drug administration than following a history of unexpected drug administration. Following the self-administration phase of the experiment, the self-administration cues are no longer followed by alcohol, and the alcohol compensatory conditional responses would result. That is precisely what Mello and Mendelson found. Measures of alcohol withdrawal symptoms (e.g., tremors, gastrointestinal symptoms) were greater following termination of expected than unexpected alcohol.

Mello and Mendelson presented the drug unexpectedly by administering it on the experimenter's schedule, rather than the subject's schedule. Another way to administer a drug unexpectedly is to administer it surreptitiously. Recall that Pavlov found that if bread were placed in the dog's stomach "so as to prevent the dog from noticing it," there were no conditional responses to aid the food's digestion. Similarly, if a drug is administered clandestinely, in a way that minimizes the ability to anticipate it, there is no opportunity for the drug-cancelling conditional response to occur, and the drug should have an especially large effect. If you "slip someone a mickey" it should have a greater effect than a voluntarily consumed mickey. An experiment with rodents demonstrating that rats show little morphine tolerance if the drug is surreptitiously administered has already been described.[3] In that experiment, rats lived in a homogenous dark and quiet environment, and (for one group) a distinctive cue was occasionally presented, and morphine was occasionally administered, but there was no relationship between the cue and drug. The morphine was simply administered surreptitiously from time to time. There was little evidence of tolerance to the analgesic effect of the drug in these rats with a history of clandestine drug administration.

Well before there were any experimental studies of surreptitious drug administration, such an administration procedure featured in a remarkable work of fiction, *The Moonstone*. *The Moonstone* was published in 1868, when Pavlov was eight years old. It was written by Wilkie Collins, a prominent Victorian novelist (and a friend of Charles Dickens). Over 60 years after its publication, T. S. Eliot described *The Moonstone* as "the first and the greatest of modern English detective novels."[4] The detective in the novel, Ezra Jennings, solves the mystery because he understood that the effects of a drug are modulated by the expectation of the drug. The drug was laudanum, a mixture of alcohol and opium freely available in Victorian England, and it was administered to the handsome and charismatic Franklin Blake on two occasions. The reason for Blake's consumption of laudanum is too elaborate to detail here and would necessitate a spoiler alert. Blake's first encounter with laudanum was inadvertent. Without his knowledge, it was slipped into his brandy as a prank. The second time Blake ingested the drug he knew he was getting it—he agreed that Jennings could give it to him as an experiment, and he would self-administer it, exactly one year after his initial drugging. Jennings knew that Blake drank "25 minims" of laudanum the first time he was involuntarily drugged, equivalent to about 15 milligrams of morphine—a dose in the range of that used for therapeutically administered oral morphine. Jennings understood that, if he wanted to achieve the same effect following the second laudanum administration that was seen the first time it was administered, the dose would have to be increased. Jennings stated:

> I shall run the risk of enlarging the dose to forty minims. On this occasion, Mr. Blake knows beforehand that he is going to take the laudanum—which is equivalent, physiologically speaking, to his having (unconsciously to himself) a certain capacity in him to resist the effects. If my view is right, a larger quantity is therefore imperatively required, this time, to repeat the results which the smaller quantity produced, last year.[5]

Wilkie Collins knew, in 1868, that drug tolerance may occur as a result of a single drug administration and may persist for a drug-free period of a full year. Most remarkably, he understood drug tolerance (the laudanum dose must be increased the second time it's administered), and he understood that such tolerance results from drug expectation ("on this occasion, Mr. Blake knows beforehand that he is going to take the laudanum"), and the reason that such expectation results in tolerance is because anticipation of the drug results in responses that lessen the drug effect (Blake's knowing beforehand that he will get the drug results in "a certain capacity in him to resist the effects"), and Blake's resistance to the effect of the drug were "unconsciously to himself."[6] That "certain capacity ... to resist the effects" of the drug are what we now know are conditional homeostatic responses. Mello and Mendelson's subjects displayed resistance to the effects of alcohol if they knew beforehand that they would get alcohol (because they self-administered it). Similarly, Blake's knowing beforehand that he would get laudanum leads to resistance to the effects of laudanum.

How did Wilkie Collins realize all this before it was "discovered" by scientists? Wilkie Collins was a laudanum user. As one biographer stated, while writing *The Moonstone*, "he began taking immense doses, not by the dram but by the glassful from a decanter."[7] It is very likely that Collins incorporated his own firsthand experiences with the drug in his work.[8]

More recently, the effects of covert drug administration have been studied in the laboratory. Volunteers were hooked up to intravenous drips. The infused substance typically was just saline, but, from time to time, without any warning, the saline infusion was replaced by a drug. The effect of this unpredictable infused drug can be compared to the effects of the drug administered in a more traditional manner.

One such intravenous administration experiment was done with the most popular drug in our culture, caffeine. Caffeine is classified as a stimulant, a drug that generally increases activity in the central nervous system. The stimulant properties of caffeine provide the "lift" that many people report when they drink coffee (and the inability to sleep if they drink it too close to bedtime). Like other stimulants, caffeine may increase blood pressure. If people who do not generally drink coffee are persuaded in the name of science to drink it, they typically will evidence an increase in blood pressure. In contrast, people who habitually consume large quantities of caffeinated coffee become tolerant to many of the effects of caffeine, including the effect on blood pressure. In one experiment, drinking coffee did, as expected, elevate blood pressure in people who were not habitual coffee drinkers, and it did not produce an elevation in blood pressure in habitual coffee drinkers.[9] Coffee aficionados have lots of pairings of a distinctively flavored beverage with the systemic effect of caffeine, and the taste of coffee causes them to expect caffeine. But what happens if these people get the drug by way of intravenous infusion, bypassing all the usual stimuli that inform the body that the drug is on the way? In this same experiment, caffeine was also administered to these coffee drinkers and coffee novices via intravenous drip, thereby bypassing the usual cues for the drug. In both methods of caffeine administration (drinking coffee and intravenous caffeine) the amount of caffeine administered was selected to result in similar blood concentrations of the stimulant. For habitual coffee drinkers, the effects of this intravenous caffeine, administered without warning, were very different than the effects of caffeine administered in coffee. Their blood pressure increased (by about the same amount seen in coffee novices) in response to the intravenous administration; there was no tolerance to the blood pressure effect of the caffeine in these experienced coffee drinkers if the caffeine was administered without warning.[10]

Similar results were obtained in an experiment concerning tolerance to an opiate drug—hydromorphone. Hydromorphone (better known by its brand name, Dilaudid) is, like heroin, a derivative of morphine. Ronald Ehrman and colleagues evaluated the effects of the drug in detoxified opiate users under two conditions: (a) when they intravenously self-administered the drug (after going through their usual "cooking up" ritual), and (b) when the drug was infused by the experimenter (via intravenous drip) without any signal. The investigators noted that several effects of hydromorphone were greater when the experimenter infused the drug than when it was self-administered, and concluded, "tolerance was observed when the subjects injected the opiate, but not when the same dose was received by unsignaled intravenous infusion."[11]

As discussed by several commentators, including the authors of the research evaluating the effects of drug expectation, there are some complications in interpreting the findings. For example, in Mello and Mendelson's study, the greater withdrawal symptoms seen following freely chosen, compared to coerced, consumption may be due to the fact that subjects drank more when they, and not the experimenter, chose when to drink (although this would not explain why the subjects were more tolerant to self-administered alcohol than experimenter-administered alcohol). The different effects of caffeine in habitual coffee drinkers when they consumed coffee versus when caffeine was administered intravenously might be a result of the slower onset of ingested caffeine, compared to intravenous caffeine.[12] To avoid such complications, researchers have turned to a procedure called the "yoked control" design.

Imagine two subjects, not in any contact with each other, participating in a drug administration experiment at the same time. During the experiment both subjects are in identical environments, and both have been prepared with intravenous lines connected to a drug-delivery device. One of the subjects arbitrarily is designated the experimental subject, and the other the yoked-control subject. There is a switch that can be pressed in both the experimental and control subjects' environments. Both subjects get a drug whenever the experimental subject presses the switch in its environment. Operation of the switch in the yoked-control subject's environment doesn't do anything. Both the experimental and yoked-control subjects receive the same doses of the drug, equally often, and at the same intervals. The only difference is that the experimental subject (but not the yoked partner) expects the drug, because it chooses to make some response that it knows will result in drug administration. Yoked-control designs of this sort have been used almost exclusively with rats.

The various yoked-control studies of drug administration differ in many details, but all have obtained similar results. The effects of the drugs are smaller in the experimental rats than in their yoked partners—that is, self-administration of a drug leads to greater drug tolerance than does passive receipt of the same amount of drug. Moreover, in some studies the experimenters evaluated withdrawal symptoms when the drug no longer was available (pressing the switch by the experimental subject no longer resulted in drug administration). Withdrawal symptoms were greater in the experimental rats than in yoked rats; self-administration leads to more withdrawal distress than passive receipt does. This consistent pattern of results has been seen in experiments using nicotine, cocaine, morphine, heroin, and alcohol.[13] In fact, although rats will avidly self-administer cocaine, their yoked partners (who received the same dose of cocaine independently of their behavior) find the cocaine aversive.[14] In summary, in rats, as in humans, the expected drug is better tolerated than the unexpected drug. Moreover, termination of drug access leads to greater drug withdrawal symptoms in rats that had previously expected the drug than in equally drug-exposed rats that had no basis to expect the drug. Greater withdrawal symptoms are correlated with a smaller response to the drug (greater drug tolerance).

Cues that lead to self-administration of a drug are not public—they are internal. Internal cues are experienced by the drug taker and are therefore not external. External cues are public—they are apparent to the drug-taker and someone observing the drug taker. In addition to internal cues that are paired with drug self-administration, the addict experiences other internal cues that signal the drug.

12 Evocative Effects of a Small Drug Dose

> Once he takes any alcohol into his system, something happens, both in the bodily and mental sense, which makes it virtually impossible for him to stop. The experience of any alcoholic will confirm that. . . . We are without defense against the first drink.
> —Anonymous, *Alcoholics Anonymous: The Story of How Many Thousands of Men and Women Have Recovered from Alcoholism* (New York: Works, 1939), 34–35

For the addict undergoing withdrawal distress, administration of the drug provides relief. The unconditional effect of the drug cancels the conditional effect. We might expect that administration of a small drug dose would provide a small amount of relief—there should be a small cancellation of the drug conditional response. However, that is not the case. Rather, administration of a small drug dose to the addict or former addict actually precipitates withdrawal symptoms and craving for the drug.

Drug-free former heroin addicts display withdrawal symptoms when they are administered a small heroin dose in a residential laboratory.[1] Similarly, alcoholics who participated in experiments during periods of abstinence displayed craving for alcohol[2] and evidence of alcohol withdrawal[3] when administered a small dose of alcohol. Cigarette smokers will display nicotine withdrawal symptoms if they receive less than the typical amount of nicotine from a cigarette (they puff on a cigarette containing less than the usual amount of nicotine).[4] The effect of a small dose of the drug in evoking withdrawal symptoms has been demonstrated in nonhumans as well as humans.[5]

The paradoxical effect of a small drug dose can be explained as follows. Experienced drug users have extensive experience with a small drug effect as a signal for a larger drug effect. An internal cue, apparent to the addict, is the early effect of a drug. With many drugs, a feeling that a substantial drug effect will imminently occur is elicited by early subjective alteration induced by the drug. The effect of a drug has a time course. A gradual increase in systemic concentration is an inevitable consequence of many drug administration procedures. The effect of the drug increases until it reaches a peak, and then gradually subsides. If this time-effect curve is gradual, and we are experienced drug takers, we can often detect the very early effects of a drug—we get an inkling that a peak drug effect is going to occur in a very short time. These drug onset cues are like a small dose of a drug, and they are paired with the later, larger drug effect. Drug onset cues, then, may act as conditional stimuli, as they are invariably paired with the subsequent peak effect of the drug. As indicated by drug researcher Andrew Goudie:

> To the extent that when any drug is administered, a reliable predictor of the presence of any specific dose will be [the] lower "functional" dose of the drug, as the drug gradually increases in body tissue after administration, it follows that drug onset may be a critical part of the CS [conditional stimulus] complex controlling the compensatory CR [conditional response].[6]

The effectiveness of drug onset cues as conditional stimuli depends on the characteristics of the time-effect curve of the drug effect. If the drug is administered via a very efficient route—a route that places the drug at the site of relevant drug receptors in the brain very quickly—we might expect that drug onset cues are not important. The peak effect of the drug occurs so quickly after administration that there is simply no time to detect an early, non-intoxicating drug effect. However, if the drug is administered via a relatively inefficient route, such that the time between administration and maximum drug effect is protracted, the small early detectable drug effect can serve as a very good signal for the impending intoxication.

One way to evaluate the effectiveness of an early small drug effect as a cue for a later, larger drug effect is to actually administer a small dose of a drug prior to a larger dose. This duplicates the small drug effect experienced before a later, larger drug effect within a single administration. An experiment by psychologists Janet Greeley and colleagues involved administering a small dose of alcohol just before administering a larger dose of alcohol.[7] Rats in one group (Paired) were injected with a low dose of alcohol 60 minutes prior to being injected with a high dose of alcohol. Another group of rats (Unpaired) received the low and high doses of alcohol on a random basis, so for these rats the low dose did not become a conditional stimulus for the high dose. When tested for the tolerance to the hypothermic effect (a decrease in body temperature) of the high dose following the low dose, Paired rats, but not Unpaired rats, displayed tolerance. Moreover, if the high dose of alcohol was not preceded by the low dose, Paired rats failed to display their usual tolerance; the high dose not followed by the usual conditional stimulus resulted in an alcohol overdose. This tolerance, dependent on an alcohol-alcohol pairing, was mediated by an ethanol-compensatory homeostatic response; Paired rats, but not Unpaired rats, evidenced a hyperthermic response (an elevation in body temperature) in response to the low dose of alcohol.

Research has been conducted with morphine that is similar to the alcohol research. If a small dose of morphine is injected prior to a large dose, is comes to serve as a conditional stimulus for the large dose and controls the display of morphine tolerance.[8] In other research morphine was administered to rats intravenously via a gradual infusion. When these rats were tested with a briefer infusion (to duplicate the earlier effect of the longer infusion), they displayed drug-compensatory learned responses (i.e., withdrawal symptoms).[9]

Because of the history of pairing of a small drug (onset) effect with a later, larger peak drug effect, small drug doses do not alleviate withdrawal effects in experienced drug users. Rather, a small drug effect, if not soon followed by large drug effect, precipitates withdrawal. The small drug effect is a signal for a larger drug effect, and, if the larger drug effect is not experienced, withdrawal symptoms result.

The "loss of control" in the abstaining alcoholic elicited by a small dose of alcohol is incorporated in the doctrine of Alcoholics Anonymous. According to Alcoholics Anonymous, the alcoholic is so sensitive to alcohol that even a small amount may precipitate relapse. Actually, the insalubrious effect of the first drink is due to the alcoholic's association of that initial effect of alcohol as a signal for the subsequent larger amounts of the drug. As pointed out by psychologist Murray Goddard, "the signal value of a small drug dose may make a contribution to 'binge' drinking and drug 'priming' effects in humans."[10] In fact, according to addiction researcher Harriet de Wit, for a variety of drugs, including opiates, "abstinent drug users often report that taking even a small amount of their previously abused drug increases their desire for the drug and can lead to a full relapse."[11] A small drug dose is one of many internal signals that prepare the addict for the full drug dose. In addition to self-administration cues and small-dose cues, there are other internal cues for a drug.

13 Images, Cognitions, and Emotions as Cues for Drugs

> A good case exists, then, for making cognitions *per se* a pivotal concern of conditioning models, allowing the possibility of cognitions as interoceptive [internal] cues.
> —Janet Greeley and Colin Ryan, "The Role of Interoceptive Cues for Drug Delivery in Conditioning Models of Drug Dependence," in *Addictive Behaviour: Cue Exposure Theory and Practice,* ed. D. Colin Drummond, Stephen T. Tiffany, Steven Glautier, and Bob Remington (New York: Wiley, 1995), 132

The experienced drug taker has internal cues associated with the drug effect as well as external cues. The internal cues are experienced only by the drug-taker (e.g., cues incidental to self-administration and the small initial effect of the drug). The external cues are apparent to the drug taker and any nearby observer (e.g., the physical environment in which the drug is administered and distinctive drug-administration ritual cues). Among additional internal cues for a drug are images, cognitions, and emotions. For the experienced drug taker merely thinking about the drug elicits drug preparation/withdrawal symptoms. The role of drug-related thoughts in withdrawal has been demonstrated in heroin addicts,[1] alcoholics,[2] and cigarette smokers.[3]

Negative emotions are frequent elicitors of withdrawal distress and relapse. Various studies found that over 75 to 85 percent of alcoholics experienced craving for alcohol when "depressed," "nervous," or "under stress,"[4] and that craving is precipitated by "non-alcohol-related events of an unpleasant nature."[5] Similar results have been found with heroin addicts.[6] The role of negative emotions in eliciting withdrawal symptoms is consistent with the conditioning analysis of addictive behavior. As we have noted, "the conditioning analysis can parsimoniously analyze the situation in terms of associative processes. If stress has been reliably associated with abusive drinking for a particular individual, then stress can function as a conditional stimulus for the elicitation of compensatory responses and craving."[7]

Addiction scientist Charles O'Brien interviewed former heroin addicts who had been drug-free for 2 to 15 months. Based on these former addict interviews, a list of stimuli that provoked "sickness and/or craving" was constructed. A typical list (ranked from most potent to least potent) was:

1. Being offered a "taste" by an old copping buddy.
2. Seeing a friend in the act of "shooting up."
3. Talking about drugs on a copping corner.
4. Standing on copping corner.
5. Seeing a successful pusher—making lots of money, envy.
6. Socially awkward situations: job interview, family criticism, feeling like an outsider at a party.
7. Talking about drugs in group therapy.
8. Seeing a few bags of heroin.
9. Seeing someone's "works."
10. See pictures of drugs and "works."

11. Seeing antidrug poster with "good veins" and somebody "shooting up."[8]

The list consists of both external stimuli ("being offered a 'taste,' "standing on a copping corner," "seeing a few bags of heroin"), and internal stimuli that remind the ex-addict of drugs ("seeing a successful pusher," "socially awkward situations," "seeing pictures of drugs"). Even the depiction of addiction-related stimuli on an anti-drug poster elicited withdrawal symptoms. Internal stimuli, as well as external stimuli, can conjure up the ghost that haunts the addict.

14   Problems with Treating Addiction

> Ultimately, considering drug-associated contexts as a factor in the development and implementation of treatment strategies is likely to improve outcomes for people with substance use disorders.
> —Mandy R. LeCocq, Patrick A. Randall, Joyce Besheer, and Nadia Chaudhri, "Considering Drug-associated Contexts in Substance Use Disorders and Treatment Development," *Neurotherapeutics* 17 (2020): 50

When you're an addict you periodically encounter situations or thoughts that elicit drug-preparatory withdrawal symptoms and find yourself readministering the drug to alleviate the symptoms. These drug-preparatory symptoms are, in fact, the ghost that haunts the addict. There is considerable evidence that these symptoms are what motivates continued drug use. They are part of the individual's homeostatic machinery. These drug preparatory symptoms are the price to be paid for minimizing the imminent pharmacological assault when the drug is delivered. It would seem like treating addiction in the addict motivated to quit would involve elimination of these preparatory conditional responses.

One way of eliminating the drug-preparatory responses that motivate continued drug use is by simply avoiding the cues that call forth these responses—that is, relocate from an area rich in these stimuli to another environment. This geographic cure, although effective, is usually not practical. Most addicts cannot relocate to a new area free of drug-associated cues.

Even if the addict stays in his or her usual environment, it seems like it should be possible to deal with the associations that have been formed between drug-paired stimuli and the drug. As already discussed, a conditional stimulus will gradually fail to exhibit a conditional response if it is repeatedly presented alone, that is, without the unconditional stimulus with which it had previously been paired. This process is termed *extinction*. A person that salivates at the sight of a lemon will gradually lose this response if they are repeatedly presented with a lemon but prevented from consuming it.[1] Treatment should consist of extinction of the association between the usual drug-associated cues and the drug. The addict should be exposed to these cues but the drug is withheld.

As a treatment for addiction, the technique of presenting the conditional stimulus, while withholding the unconditional stimulus, to gradually weaken the connection between the two was known to Shakespeare. In *Hamlet*, act 3, scene 4, Hamlet's advice to his mother for treating her addiction to his uncle indicates an appreciation of extinction:

> Assume a virtue, if you have it not . . .
> Refrain tonight,
> And that shall lend a kind of easiness
> To the next abstinence; the next more easy;
> For use almost can change the stamp of nature.

The extinction therapy for addiction requires that the addict "assume a virtue." He or she must confront drug-paired cues, experience the drug-preparatory conditional response, and "refrain" from drug administration. The ghost of addiction is repeatedly summoned and repeatedly ignored. As this is done over and over, the successive abstinences will become less pronounced—that is, "more easy."

Exposing patients to drug-associated cues that elicit craving and withdrawal distress is generally considered taboo in most treatment environments. However, protecting patients from exposure to drug-associated cues is likely to be counterproductive. As noted by some addiction researchers, "this overprotective practice is unfortunate, because many patients retain cue reactivity, that is, powerful physiological reactions to drug-related stimuli, even after significant treatment."[2]

Extinction therapy for the addict is termed "cue exposure."[3] Exposing the addict to drug predictive cues, in a situation in which there is no drug availability, would be expected to extinguish the drug-preparatory responses that are withdrawal symptoms. There are many studies evaluating cue exposure as a treatment for excessive use of licit and illicit drugs by humans, including alcohol, nicotine, cocaine, and opiates. Generally, the treatment, conducted in a clinical setting, consists of having the addict think about drug-administration scenarios, presenting pictures of drug stimuli, and perhaps having the addict interact with the paraphernalia of addiction (e.g., hypodermic syringes and spoons for cooking up drug for heroin addicts, alcohol bottles and shot glasses for alcoholics, and cigarette packs and matches for smokers). Although there are reports that cue-exposure treatment is effective, the findings are mixed—that is, there also are reports that such treatment is ineffective, or effective with some drugs but not with others, or effective only as an adjunct to more traditional treatments, or effective with some addicts but not with others.[4] In the words of Yale addiction researcher Kathleen M. Carroll: "While cue exposure approaches have generally been associated with reductions in some conditioned responses, the value of these procedures in producing clinically meaningful reductions in substance use has been met with only modest success to date."[5]

If withdrawal symptoms are learned responses elicited by drug-paired stimuli, why isn't extinction of this association generally recognized as an effective therapy? One problem is that the repeated elicitation of withdrawal symptoms is so aversive that patient compliance is a problem. The patient, when repeatedly confronted with drug-associated stimuli not culminating in drug administration, simply drops out of treatment. Another problem with cue-exposure treatment is its short duration. The addict has, in most cases, many years of experience in pairing drug-predictive cues with the systemic effect of the drug. The association is very strong because it is so well practiced. The relatively brief period of cue-exposure therapy would not be expected to extinguish such a well-entrenched conditional response. Another reason that cue exposure is not generally recognized as effective is because the cue-exposure therapist does not appreciate the need to extinguish all of the multitude of external and internal cues that have been paired with the drug. Typically, cue-exposure treatment involves exposure of drug-associated, external environmental cues to patients who have self-administered drugs. However, cue exposure, to be effective, must consist of extinction of internal cues as well as the plethora of exteroceptive cues.

The fact that internal cues culminating in self-administration function as highly salient drug-predictive stimuli has important implications for cue exposure treatments. If self-administration is an important predictor of drug effects, effective extinction treatments should incorporate opportunities for the patient to engage in the behaviors that previously had culminated in drug administration. According to Spanish psychiatrist Adolf Tobeña and his colleagues:

> It can also be useful to consider the possibility that controlling for the direct consequences of self-administration of drugs (e.g., drinking or injecting), could affect the extinction of the affective states induced by drugs or drug cues . . . treatment should incorporate specific strategies for dealing with the behavioral chains involved in drinking, inhaling, smoking or self-injecting drugs. The corresponding prediction would be that the practice of such behavioral rituals while the patients are exposed to cues (but without actual intake of drugs), would lead to faster extinction and loss of the signal value of such behaviors as cues for the drugs.[6]

The early effect of the drug is inevitably paired with the subsequent peak effect, and another internal cue is the small drug that signals the later, larger drug effect. Giving the drug addict small doses of the drug during treatment is anathema to some treatment programs, but it is an important drug-paired cue to be extinguished. According to addiction researcher Antonio Cepeda-Benito, "the inclusion of small drug doses during cue exposure treatments may better reproduce the CSs [conditional stimuli] responsible for craving."[7] Giving alcoholics small doses of alcohol as part of treatment is contra-indicated in traditional alcohol treatments (e.g., Alcoholics Anonymous), which claim that the small doses would precipitate relapse to alcohol use. However, some investigators described successful cue-exposure treatment procedures for problem drinking that incorporate small doses of alcohol.[8]

It is particularly difficult to extinguish the cognitive and emotional cues for a drug. Nevertheless, if an addict has a history of self-administration when under stress, then cue exposure should involve extinguishing the association with stress and drug use. There have been attempts to expose the addict to stressful cues during cue exposure. These attempts usually determine stressful events that are paired with drug use in an initial interview, then have the client recapitulate these events during cue exposure treatment.[9] Alternatively, the therapist may ask the patient to imagine a past or potential future emotionally challenging event, such as sadness (imagining the death of a loved one) or anger (imagining dispute with spouse).[10]

Even if cue-exposure therapy involves extinction of all the cues associated with drug use, both external and internal, there is another complication in using cue exposure to treat addiction. A view of extinction as *unlearning*—an eradication of the association formed during acquisition—is pervasive and is implicit in most implementations of cue-exposure therapy. We now know that's not the case. In fact, Pavlov demonstrated that extinction of a response did not mean that it was eradicated. The association learned prior to extinction is intact, even after extinction. All that is necessary for an extinguished learned response to reappear is the passage of time. In the words of Pavlov, "left to themselves, extinguished conditioned reflexes spontaneously recover their full strength after a longer or shorter interval of time."[11] Following Pavlov, the reappearance of an extinguished response after a period of time has elapsed after extinction is complete is termed "spontaneous recovery." In common with other preparatory learned responses, the preparatory responses that are responsible for drug tolerance and chronic withdrawal display spontaneous recovery, and complicate cue-exposure treatment. For example, chronic alcohol tolerance results from an alcohol-compensatory conditional response. Although such tolerance may be extinguished by repeated presentation of alcohol-associated cues, the tolerant response reappears after an interval had been allowed to elapse. Alcohol tolerance, which had been extinguished, returned when rats were tested 24 days after the completion of extinction.[12] Similarly, humans display substantial spontaneous recovery of completely extinguished learned preparatory responses.[13]

With few exceptions, spontaneous recovery has not been recognized as a complication of cue-exposure treatment. To minimize the magnitude of spontaneous recovery, cue-exposure treatment should use widely spaced extinction trials and should include re-extinction sessions in which the spontaneously recovered preparatory drug response may be repeatedly extinguished.[14]

Results of research conducted in the past 40 years clearly indicate that extinction does not entail the loss of prior learning. An extensive series of experiments, primarily by psychologists Mark Bouton and colleagues, indicate that, just as something is learned during acquisition (the relationship between the usual drug-paired cues and the drug), something also is learned during extinction (a conflicting relationship between the usual drug-paired cues and the *absence* of the drug). During extinction, the association learned during acquisition remains intact, while the new, conflicting association is acquired. Once you've learned something you are permanently changed. Once you have learned to associate cues with a drug effect, you cannot unlearn it; You cannot un-ring the bell with extinction trials. Rather, according to Bouton, "the signal winds up with two available 'meanings.' It is ambiguous . . . its current meaning—or the behavior it currently evokes—is determined by the current context."[15]

Most cue-exposure treatments are conducted in a clinical setting. The patient is exposed to cues associated with drug use, and the drug is withheld, in a setting very different from that in which drug addiction actually occurs. At the end of cue-exposure therapy, the individual might appear to be "cured"; he or she does not display drug-preparatory withdrawal symptoms when confronted with drug-paired stimuli. However, the original learning that established this association is still present and is expressed when the cue-exposure-treated patient returns to the environment in which this original learning was established.

In one experiment rats were trained to press a lever in a distinctive context for alcohol reward. They then were extinguished in a different context—lever presses no longer delivered alcohol, and they stopped responding for the drug. When these rats were placed back in the original distinctive context, even though alcohol was no longer available, they continued to lever press at a high rate for several weeks.[16]

In an attempt to extinguish drug-associated stimuli in the addiction environment there have been some attempts to conduct cue-exposure therapy in the field, rather than in the clinic. For example, in a study of cue exposure for alcoholism, the therapist and the patient together reviewed the stimuli associated with excessive drinking, and a yeoman's effort was made to duplicate these stimuli as closely as possible during treatment (e.g., the alcoholic patient and therapist would go together to the pub where the alcoholic habitually drank and would drink only soft drinks).[17] Most of the patients (five out of the six patients) attained abstinence from drinking by the end of therapy, and this abstinence was maintained over follow-ups of up to nine months.

Recently there have been reports of successful cue-exposure treatment using virtual reality. The addict is presented with computer-generated scenes designed to duplicate the addict's confrontation with addiction-related cues in the environment is which these cues naturally occur.[18]

Finally, there is a caution that must be exercised when using cue-exposure treatment. If the therapy is successful, the patient no longer displays conditional responses to drug-predictive cues. These cues no longer call forth withdrawal symptoms that motivate continued drug use, but they no longer produce the drug-predictive responses that can protect the addict from overdose. If the post-treatment addict returns to drug use, he or she may overdose. Indeed, following "successful" treatment the newly discharged addict is at a heightened risk of overdose, thus treatment may have counterproductive effects.[19]

15 The Special Case of Cigarettes

> A cigarette is the perfect type of a perfect pleasure. It is exquisite, and it leaves one unsatisfied. What more can one want?
> —Oscar Wilde, *The Picture of Dorian Gray* (Peterborough, ON: Broadview Press, 1998 [1890]), 116

A widespread addiction in our culture is addiction to cigarettes. A 2020 research article by physician and nicotine researcher Prabhat Jha reported that 14 percent of the adult population smokes (a decrease from the 50 percent who smoked before the 1964 Surgeon General's report on the link between smoking and lung cancer).[1] Cigarettes are readily available, portable, and legal. It's so easy to smoke a cigarette that, unless deprived of cigarettes, the addictive nature of the habit is not readily apparent. Only when the smoker tries to give up the habit is the addictive nature of smoking revealed. The smoker who abstains from cigarettes experiences extreme withdrawal symptoms and craving. The following example highlights the addictive nature of cigarettes and the consequences of restrictions on the supply of cigarettes. Following World War II cigarettes were rationed in Germany: two packs per month for men and one pack per month for women. In 1948 Dr. F. I.

Arntzen, of Münster, Germany, reported the effects of this postwar cigarette famine:

> Up to a point, the majority of habitual smokers preferred to do without food even under extreme conditions of nutrition rather than forgo tobacco. Thus when food rations in prisoner of war camps were down to 900–1000 calories, smokers were still willing to barter their food rations for tobacco. Of 300 German civilians questioned, 256 had obtained tobacco at the black market. . . . Many housewives who were smokers bartered fat and sugar for cigarettes. In disregard of considerations of personal dignity, conventional decorum, and esthetic-hygienic feelings, cigarette butts were picked out of street dirt by people who, in their own statements, would in any other circumstances have felt disgust at such contact. Smokers also condescended to beg for tobacco, but not for other things. . . . In reports of subjective impressions, 80% of those questioned declared that it felt worse to do without nicotine than without alcohol.[2]

Smoking is unique among addictive substances. The addictive chemical, nicotine, is inhaled, and quickly reaches receptor cells in the brain. It takes about 7 seconds for inhaled nicotine to get from the lungs to the brain—faster than it takes for heroin injected into the arm to get to the brain. Most cigarette users smoke a pack or more a day (less than 8 percent of smokers smoke about one cigarette per day).[3] In the words of cigarette researcher Michael Russell:

> At 10 puffs per cigarette, the pack-a-day smoker gets more than 70,000 nicotine shots to his brain in a year. It is hardly surprising that cigarette smoking is so addictive. . . . Indeed, cigarette smoking is probably the most addictive and dependence-producing form of object-specific self-administered gratification known to man. . . . This simply means that, throughout history, no other single biologically unnecessary object has meant so much to so many people who, after a few initiating experiences, have needed to have it so often and so regularly, for so many years, despite

trying so hard to do without it; and for which there is no other adequate substitute.[4]

The addicted cigarette smoker indulges in his or her habit in many different contexts and is largely unfettered by legal constraints on environmental cue/nicotine pairings. About 68 percent of smokers say they would like to quit.[5] Most attempt to quit but soon relapse. The smoker gets several hundred drug administrations a day and has many pairings of a variety of stimuli with the drug. Although there are increasingly limited places where cigarettes can be smoked, there remain many different places in the home, the work environment, and the car that become associated with the effects of nicotine. Each administration of nicotine is rewarding; each puff has beneficial cognitive effects on attention and memory.[6]

In addition, the many external places and internal states that accompany smoking elicit conditional nicotine-compensatory conditional responses—nicotine withdrawal symptoms. The smoker merely has to light up again to counter these symptoms. Nicotine addiction is unique among the addictions in the wide variety of stimuli that are paired with the drug effect. Each of these many different stimuli become paired with a shot of nicotine many thousands of times. When the cigarette smoker tries to abstain, each of these many stimuli will conjure up ghosts that haunt the person trying to stop smoking.

16 Why Doesn't Everyone Become an Addict?

> Addiction is something believed to be happening to others. . . . The fact that drugs seem to be the pleasure of many and the doom of just a few "others" contributes strongly to the difficulty in controlling and forbidding drug use at the societal level.
> —Pier V. Piazza and Veronique Deroche-Gamonet, "A Multistep General Theory of Transition to Addiction," *Psychopharmacology* 229 (2013): 388

The popular view of the heroin user is someone enslaved by their habit. They go to great lengths, at considerable cost to health and finances, to satisfy their craving for the drug. The widely held belief that any nonmedical use of opiates usually leads to addiction ("it's so good, don't even try it once") is incorrect.

It is generally recognized that, for drug use to be categorized as addictive, it must meet certain criteria. Generally recognized criteria are those outlined in the latest (fifth) edition of *The Diagnostic and Statistical Manual of Mental Disorders*, the gold-standard text of the American Psychiatric Association. To be an addict you must use the substance more often than intended, and you want to decrease or eliminate your use of the drug, but you cannot. The drug use causes you to neglect responsibilities and relationships, and you use the drug in settings that are risky. Finally, you have tolerance to the drug and display withdrawal symptoms when you don't use the drug.

It's surprising to many people to know that most drug users (except for cigarette smokers) do not fit the mold of the addict. Most of the people who self-administer opiates use the drug recreationally, but not habitually.[1] As few as 10 percent of nonmedical opiate users are "addicted."[2] This is approximately the same as the percentage of people who drink alcohol that are "alcoholic."[3] Most drug and alcohol users use the substance as a form of relaxation, as a way of unwinding, as a social lubricant, and a pleasant interlude in their daily activities. These nonaddicted individuals schedule their drug use so that it does not interfere with work or family obligations.

The use of drugs by these recreational drug users was exemplified by Wilkie Collins, the Victorian novelist who used laudanum (which was not yet illegal) while a productive writer. Laudanum was used for its beneficial effects, not because it countered withdrawal symptoms. As one of the characters in his 1864 novel, *Armadale*, stated:

> Who was the man who invented laudanum? I thank him from the bottom of my heart, whoever he was. If all the miserable wretches in pain of body and mind, whose comforter he has been, could meet together to sing his praises, what a chorus it would be. I have had six delicious hours of oblivion; I have woke up with my mind composed. . . . I have drunk my cup of tea with real relish of it; I have dawdled over my morning toilet with an exquisite sense of relief—and all through the modest little bottle of drops I see on my chimney piece at this moment. "Drops" you are a darling! If I love nothing else, I love you.[4]

Most users are recreational users and typically they do not create problems with their drug use. They do not spend all their income to obtain the drug, they do not routinely become intoxicated, they do not engage in antisocial activities when obtaining or using the drug, and they tend not to engage with anti-drug authorities. Carl Hart, Professor of Psychology (and former Chair of the Psychology Department) at Columbia University has written persuasively about the nonaddictive use of a variety of illicit drugs.[5] Society is concerned with addicts—not recreational drug users.

What accounts for the individual differences in addiction vulnerability? In all of us the drug effect elicits homeostatic corrections; we associate drug-predictive cues with the drug effect and experience anticipatory drug homeostatic corrections ("withdrawal symptoms") in the presence of drug-predictive cues. These phenomena are responsible for chronic tolerance (thereby protecting the individual from overdose) as well as chronic withdrawal symptoms (which are alleviated by drug acquisition). But here is an important distinction: Although we all similarly respond to drug administration, we don't all become addicted.

There are research studies that have attempted to ascertain which individuals are, and are not, likely to become addicts, and they have reached a similar conclusion. Individuals who are at risk for addiction are minimally affected by the drug when it is initially administered. For example, young people who seem to not respond to alcohol are at the greatest risk for future problem drinking. Psychiatrist Marc Schuckit has extensively investigated individual differences in susceptibility to alcoholism. In his studies, many young men, with and without a family history of alcoholism (but not yet alcohol dependent), were challenged with alcohol. They drank a beverage containing a measured amount of alcohol in the laboratory, and effects of the alcohol were assessed with many physiological measures and subjective measures of intoxication. These participants were followed for the next several decades. Those who displayed a low level of response to the alcohol challenge subsequently tended to abuse alcohol: "a lower sensitivity to modest doses of alcohol is associated with a significant increase in the risk of future alcoholism, perhaps through increasing the chances that a person will drink more heavily and more often."[6] That is, according to Schuckit, the apparent lower sensitivity to alcohol causes people to consume more of it. Rats, too, who are apparently relatively insensitive to alcohol are more likely to voluntarily consume alcohol.[7] Similarly, research on susceptibility to morphine addiction in rats indicates that those animals that show a small response to the analgesic effects of the drug are especially likely to become avid self-administrators.[8]

A small response to a drug may, as Schuckit suggests, indicate that the addiction-prone individuals are insensitive to the drug. There is, however, an alternative explanation. A small response to the drug would result if the drug-induced disturbance produced an especially large homeostatic corrective response. According to this interpretation, the addiction-prone individual experiences both the effect of the drug and a large-drug cancelling compensatory response. The potential alcoholic does not display a minimal response to alcohol because they are "insensitive" to the drug, but rather because they are *hypersensitive* to the drug—they respond to the drug-induced disturbance with an exaggerated homeostatic drug-compensatory response that largely cancels the drug effect.

We now know that the latter explanation is correct. As a result of their genetic predisposition, people differ in the strength of their homeostatic correction to a drug-induced disturbance. People with a large drug-compensatory response display a small response to the drug because the direct effect of the drug is greatly attenuated by a large corrective response.[9] They display a large homeostatic correction when initially challenged with the drug (accounting for acute tolerance), and thus a large anticipatory homeostatic correction when confronted by drug-associated cues (accounting for chronic tolerance).

It is reasonable to suppose that addiction liability is related to the magnitude of the compensatory drug response. Those individuals who respond to the drug with an especially large homeostatic correction should have an especially profound "withdrawal" response elicited by drug-predictive cues and be especially motivated to seek drugs to lessen the withdrawal response. Thus, individuals who are minimally responsive to the drug should be especially likely to become addicted.

If a small response to a drug results from a large compensatory response, we would expect to see an especially profound conditional response to drug-predictive cues in those individuals who display a small drug response. This has been confirmed with respect to alcohol. Those individuals who display a small intoxicating response to alcohol display an especially large response to alcohol-associated cues.[10] In summary, those individuals who are especially at risk for addiction have particularly robust homeostatic responses to the drug. Thus, cues associated with drug administration elicit strong drug-compensatory responses. The person at risk for addiction has exceptionally strong drug-withdrawal symptoms.

Not everyone with an exaggerated drug-compensatory response will become an addict. Most people who show a minimal response to a drug because their drug-compensatory response is large manage to avoid addiction simply by putting up with the large withdrawal response, or sometimes by opting for abstinence. Others who do not have an exaggerated drug compensatory response will become addicts because they belong to a subculture that endorses the rituals of obtaining and using drugs.[11] Nevertheless, the individual who is minimally responsive to the drug is at risk for addiction.

17 Does Addiction Result in Brain Damage?

If early voluntary drug use goes undetected and unchecked, the resulting changes in the brain can ultimately erode a person's ability to control the impulse to take addictive drugs.
—Nora D. Volkow, George F. Koob, and A. Thomas McLellan, "Neurobiologic Advances from the Brain Disease Model of Addiction," *New England Journal of Medicine* 374 (2016): 369

The model of brain disease in addiction, as currently formulated, is simple, biased, profit-seeking, reductionist, not based on the existing scientific data on addiction or on the biosocial model, and, moreover, it does not serve the interest of consumers or addicts.
—Elisardo Becoña, "Brain Disease or Biopsychosocial Model in Addiction? Remembering the Vietnam Veteran Study," *Psicothema* 30 (2018): 273

Insights into addiction provided by Benjamin Rush and Robert Macnish in the nineteenth century (before drug use was restricted) and Lawrence Kolb in the early part of the twentieth century (at the start of the period of anti-drug legislation) all indicate that drug-associated cues are crucial to drug addiction. Hundreds of years of addiction study leads to a simple conclusion: the addict has learned something that the nonaddict hasn't learned. That is the primary distinction between the addict and the nonaddict.

The addict has learned that certain cues are paired with a drug. He or she is probably unaware of this learning because Pavlovian conditioning can proceed without awareness, but this learning is the inevitable result of the pairing of events. The learning is adaptive. Chronic drug tolerance is crucially dependent on this learning. The addict is likely to endure even a high dose of the drug if the drug is administered in the usual drug-administration environment.

Those individuals who are genetically predisposed to have an exaggerated drug-induced homeostatic correction, who therefore come to respond to the drug-paired cues with a large conditional drug response, are the most uncomfortable if they are in the presence of stimuli that have been paired with the drug. These individuals are at the most risk of addiction. The adaptive conditional responses that prepare the addict for the next drug administration by minimizing the effect of the drug are pronounced. The ghost that haunts the addict is the most profound with these people with a large homeostatic drug response.

The fact that addiction is a learning phenomenon means that the brains of drug users are different than those who don't use drugs. The brain of the user is different in the sense that the brain of someone who has learned to salivate at the sight of a lemon, or to ride an escalator without falling, is different from that of someone who hasn't had the necessary pairings. The brains of drug users are different as a result of their conditioning history—not damaged, just different.

There is another view of addiction—one that has gained considerable traction in recent years. According to this view, addiction is not an adaptive response. Rather, it is a brain disease. According to Alan Leshner, the former head of the major U.S. addiction research funding agency, the National Institute on Drug Abuse, "A metaphorical switch in the brain seems to be thrown as a result of prolonged drug use.... An addict's brain is different from a nonaddict's brain, and the addicted individual must be dealt with as if he or she is in a different brain state."[1] Leshner's article was titled "Addiction Is a Brain Disease, and It Matters." It invited controversy, as revealed by a rejoinder article, "Addiction Is Not a Brain Disease (and It Matters),"[2] but it has been very influential in setting the research agenda of the National Institute on Drug Abuse. As summarized by neuroscientist Marc Lewis, "the brain disease model is the most prevalent model of addiction in the western world. Particularly in the United States, it dominates professional and public discourse on prevention, treatment, research agendas, and policy issues."[3] (Lewis's article is titled "Brain Change in Addiction as Learning, Not Disease"). According to this most prevalent brain disease model, the addict is not likely to relapse simply because he or she is in the presence of cues than have been paired with drug use. Rather, the damaged brain is responsible for continued drug use. As a result of taking drugs, the drug-user has a diseased brain, which compels the user to seek out drugs.

The brain-disease model does acknowledge that an association forms between drug-paired cues and the drug effect, but this association develops when the brain-damaged addict is compelled to use drugs. The association between drug-paired cues and the drug effect is considered to be a further manifestation of the brain-damaged addict's pathology. There is no consideration that this association may be an adaptive response that protects the drug-taker from the effects of a high dose of the drug.

Researchers committed to this brain-damage model of addiction have reported many brain-neuroimaging studies that, using colorful pictures of the brain, purport to show the abnormal nature of the addict's brain—the damage that causes the addict to seek drugs. These pictures are obtained from studies using sophisticated brain-imaging procedures: magnetic resonance imaging (MRI), functional MRI (fMRI), and positron-emission tomography (PET). Implicit in these brain imaging studies is the view that addiction is a disease of the brain, in the way that Parkinson's disease or amyotrophic lateral sclerosis (ALS, or Lou Gehrig's disease) are diseases of the brain. However, Parkinson's and ALS are unambiguous on brain scans. That's not the case for an addict's brain scan.

Advocates of the brain-disease model of addiction concentrate on brain-imaging studies showing positive findings and minimize findings that fail to replicate results. For example, several studies reported enlarged brain regions in drug-dependent individuals compared to non-drug users, but others found a *reduction* in the size of these areas in the drug users. Still others have found no structural abnormalities in the addicts.[4] The research on brain changes resulting from drug use is also subject to numerous methodological challenges.[5] There is considerable overlap in images of the brain of drug users and non-users. If the brain scans of users and non-users were mixed together it would be nearly impossible to correctly identify which scans belonged to users and which to non-users.[6] Nevertheless, politicians tasked with funding addiction research are impressed by colorful brain images. Bob Schuster, head of the National Institute on Drug Abuse from 1986 to 1991, admitted capitalizing on the brain disease model of addiction. He acknowledged that although he did not subscribe to the model, he was "happy for it to be conceptualized that way for pragmatic reasons . . . for selling it to congress."[7]

Evidence contrary to the brain-disease model of addiction are findings of the limited career of most addicts. Opiate addicts, if they survive long enough, tend to give up their addiction. There are many young addicts, but few elderly ones. Addicts tend to "mature out" of their addiction, giving up their drug use in their thirties.[8] If addiction is due to a brain disease, the brain would have to miraculously cure itself.

The most compelling evidence against a brain-damage interpretation of addiction comes from the profound effect of environmental manipulations on drug seeking. If the addict's drug acquisition is due to a diseased brain, why does relocation away from the addiction environment (the geographic cure) promote abstinence? Why didn't most heroin-addicted returning Vietnam veterans continue their drug use in the United States? Drug use stopped following relocation to a new environment, usually when there was no addiction treatment undertaken after moving. The addict should take his or her damaged brain to the new environment. The damaged brain should cause drug use in the new environment, as well as in the original addiction environment, but it didn't.

A letter to the prestigious journal *Nature*, signed by 94 addiction scientists, criticized the brain-disease model of addiction.[9] Despite evidence contrary to the model, it has inspired appalling acts. Philippine president Rodrigo Duterte has been responsible for the killing of tens of thousands of illegal drug users since 2016. He has justified his actions by appealing to the brain-disease model of addiction. With respect to addiction to the most abused drug in the Philippines, the stimulant drug methamphetamine, Duterte claims that methamphetamine "would adversely affect a person's brain and could induce its users to harm even their loved ones.... [M]any of the drug users become dysfunctional, some of them even beyond redemption." He elaborated: "As a matter of fact, it's an American forensic study [says] that it shrinks the brain of a person."[10] The brain-disease model has also inspired radical surgery. About 1,000 opiate-addicted patients in China were subjected to surgery between 2000 and 2004 that removed the parts of their brain that presumably were damaged from drug use. The surgery was found to have adverse effects and to be unwarranted, and was halted by China's Ministry of Health in 2004.[11]

In summary, it's not a damaged brain that is responsible for the addict's relapse to drug use. It is the conditional response to drug paired cues—the ghost that haunts the addict.

18 To Be Addicted

> Learning is one of the physiological mechanisms that give the body its wisdom.
> —Barry R. Dworkin, *Learning and Physiological Regulation*
> (Chicago: University of Chicago Press, 1993), 185

We may think our behaviors are voluntary and an expression of our free will, but we have some behaviors that that are automatic, mindless, and machine-like. These behaviors consist of reflexes that arise every day when physiological disturbances that interfere with the constancy necessary for our survival occur. These disturbances are detected and send neural impulses to the brain. The brain in turn sends impulses to receptors to initiate activity that alleviates the effect of the disturbance. This reflex activity occurs without our conscious participation. We automatically respond to certain stimuli with certain responses. We cannot *not* respond reflexively. These responses to a biologically significant stimulus are homeostatic corrections for the effects of the stimulus. As discussed by Claude Bernard and Walter Cannon, these involuntary homeostatic reflexes keep us healthy in the face of constant environmental challenges to our stability.

One disturbance that can initiate reflex activity is the effect of a drug. Many drugs cause widespread changes to our physiology, some of which threaten our survival. These drug-induced changes stimulate reflex activities that are homeostatic responses; they lessen the potentially harmful effects of the drug.

We may repeatedly take the drug. In such a case, the distinctive cues that are part of the drug-administration ritual become associated with the drug effect. Following the findings of Pavlov, the reflex activity elicited by the drug becomes elicited by these cues in anticipation of the drug effect. The homeostatic response to the drug gets bigger and bigger over the course of successive administrations because the drug-induced homeostatic reflex activity is supplemented by the anticipatory homeostatic activity elicited by drug-paired cues. Drug users have learned (usually unconsciously) to associate drug-paired cues with the effect of the drug. The anticipatory homeostatic correction is responsible for chronic tolerance. Even if the addict eventually takes a very high dose of the drug these enhanced corrective responses likely save the addict's life. If the addict takes a large dose of the drug in the presence of cues that have not been paired with the drug, he or she is at risk for drug overdose.

Drug-paired cues serve to inform the addict that the drug effect is imminent. If the addict doesn't have any information that the drug effect will be experienced, he or she cannot make the anticipatory homeostatic response that is responsible for chronic tolerance. Thus, if a drug is administered unpredictably, for example by coerced or surreptitious administration, there is little chronic tolerance.

The anticipatory drug responses are a manifestation of the wisdom of the body. An anticipatory homeostatic response can be a life-saver, but at a cost. Consider the situation when the addict is abstaining from drugs but encounters drug-paired cues (e.g., the place where he normally shot up). The drug-preparatory response occurs as an automatic reflex. The cue-elicited preparation for the drug is the ghost that haunts the addict. The abstaining addict is preparing for a drug-induced physiological perturbation, but there is no such perturbation. In such circumstances the drug-preparatory responses are mislabeled drug-withdrawal symptoms. They are uncomfortable and motivate renewed drug administration to lessen the effect of the symptoms.

The adaptive significance of chronic drug tolerance is obvious. It means we can take large drug doses without suffering ill effects, as long as the drug's effect is predictable. It's predictable either because we get the drug following the usual drug-paired cues, or we choose to self-administer the drug (rather than passively receive the drug). This chronic drug tolerance is due to an anticipatory drug response. If we're trying to abstain, we wish that we wouldn't experience the anticipatory drug response—it's the ghost that haunts the former drug user and often triggers relapse. However, we can't have the beneficial effects of chronic drug tolerance without being visited by this ghost.

Addicts don't have a brain disease as a result of drug use, despite the enthusiasm for the brain-disease view by researchers at the National Institute on Drug Abuse. They have a healthy and adaptive homeostatic response to the physiological upheaval produced by the drug. As stated in 1973 by physiologist Leroy Langley, "any paper published today, at least in physiology, which is worth the paper it is printed in, should further clarify a homeostatic mechanism."[1] The study of drug addiction provides further clarification of a homeostatic mechanism. The ghost in the addict is the evidence of this homeostatic mechanism.

Notes

Preface and Acknowledgments

1. Siegel, S. (1972). Conditioning of insulin-induced glycemia. *Journal of Comparative and Physiological Psychology, 78*(2), 233–241.

2. Siegel, S. (1975). Evidence from rats that morphine tolerance is a learned response. *Journal of Comparative and Physiological Psychology, 89*(5), 498–506.

3. Subtitled "The Overdose Explanation Is a Myth," the article was based on Brecher's book *Licit and Illicit Drugs* (Boston: Little, Brown, 1972), especially a chapter titled "The Heroin Overdose Mystery."

4. Darke, S. (2016). Heroin overdose. *Addiction,* 111(11), 260–263, at 261.

5. Siegel, S., Hinson, R. E., Krank, M. D. & McCully, J. (1982). Heroin "overdose" death: The contribution of drug-associated environmental cues. *Science, 216*(4544), 436–437.

6. Hinson, R. E., & Siegel, S. (1982). Nonpharmacological bases of drug tolerance and dependence. *Journal of Psychosomatic Research, 26*(5), 495–503, at 499.

7. Volkow, N. D., Gordon, J. A., & Koob, G. F. (2021). Choosing appropriate language to reduce the stigma around mental illness and substance use disorders, *Neuropsychopharmacology, 46*(13), 2230–2232.

8. Cannon, W. B. (1932). *The wisdom of the body.* New York: Norton.

Chapter 1

1. Greenberg, B. L. (1989). This happens from time to time. In *The Never-Not Sonnets*. Orlando: University of Central Florida Press, 25.

2. Zhao, M., Fan, C., Du, J., Jiang, H., & Sun, H. (2012). Cue induced craving and physiological reactions in recently and long-abstinent heroin-dependent patients. *Addictive Behavior, 37*(4), 393–398.

3. Cibin, M. (1993). Craving: Physiopathology and clinical aspects. *Alcologia, 5*, 257–260.

4. Biernacki, P. (1988). *Pathways from heroin addiction: Recovery without treatment*. Philadelphia: Temple University Press, 1988, 11.

5. Quoted in Mendelson, J., and Mello, N. (1985). *The diagnosis and treatment of alcoholism*. New York: McGraw-Hill, 10.

6. Curtis, W. (2007). *And a bottle of rum: A history of the New World in ten cocktails*. New York: Three Rivers Press.

7. Rush, B. (1805). *Medical inquiries and observations* (Vol. 1). Philadelphia: J. Conrad and Company, 380.

8. Rush, *Medical inquiries and observations*, 381

Chapter 2

1. MacInnes, C. (1967). Leaves of grass (review of G. Andrews and S. Vinkenoor, *The book of grass*). *Encounter, 28*, 67–70, at 67.

2. Black, J. R. (1889). Advantages of substituting the morphia habit for the incurably alcoholic. *Cincinnati Lancet-Clinic, 22*, 537–541, at 538.

3. Alston, L. J., Dupré, R., & Nonnenmacher, T. (2002). Social reformers and legislation: The prohibition of cigarettes in the United States and Canada. *Explorations in Economic Theory, 39*(4), 425–445; Troyer, R. J., &, G. E. (1983). *Cigarettes: The battles over smoking*. New Brunswick, NJ: Rutgers University Press.

4. United States Office of the Commissioner of Internal Revenue. (1915). *Treasury decisions under internal revenue laws of the United States,*

Vol 16, January-December, 1914. Washington, DC: U. S. Government Printing Office, 291.

5. Kolb, L. (1927). Clinical contribution to drug addiction: The struggle for cure and the conscious reasons for relapse. *Journal of Nervous and Mental Disease, 66,* 22–43, at 39.

6. Kolb, Clinical contribution to drug addiction, 40.

7. Kolb, Clinical contribution to drug addiction, 28.

8. Quoted in Campbell, N. D., Olsen, J. P., & Walden, L. (2008). *The narcotic farm: The rise and fall of America's first prison for drug addicts.* New York: Abrams, 15.

9. For a description of the Narcotic Farm, see Campbell, Olsen, & Walden, *The narcotic farm.*

10. Dole, V. P. (1977). Addiction: A seeming unwisdom of the body. In S. N. Pradhan & S. N. Dutta (Eds.), *Drug abuse: Clinical and basic aspects* (pp. xi–xii). Saint Louis, MO: Mosby, xi.

Chapter 3

1. Milloy, M. S., Kerr, T., Tyndall, M., Montaner, J., & Wood, E. (2008). Estimated drug overdose deaths averted by North America's first medically-supervised safer injection facility. *PLOS One, 3,* e3351. Retrieved from http://journals.plos.org/plosone/article?id=10.1371/journal.pone.0003351

2. Brecher, E. M. (1972). *Licit and illicit drugs.* Boston: Little, Brown, 110.

3. Darke, S. (2016). Addiction classics: Heroin overdose. *Addiction, 111*(11), 2060–2063, at 2061.

4. Gerevich, J., Bácskai, E., Farkas, L., & Danics, Z. (2005, July 25). A case report: Pavlovian conditioning as a risk factor of heroin "overdose" death. *Harm Reduction Journal, 2,* Article 10.1186/1477-7517-2-11. Retrieved November 13, 2012, from http://www.harmreductionjournal.com/content/2/1/11

5. Darke, S., & Zador, D. (1996). Fatal heroin "overdose:" A review. *Addiction, 91*(12), 1765–1772.

6. Monforte, J. R. (1977). Some observations concerning blood morphine concentrations in narcotic addicts. *Journal of Forensic Sciences, 22*(4), 718–724, at 720.

7. Helpern, M., & Rho, Y.-M. (1967). Deaths from narcotism in New York City: Incidence, circumstances, and postmortem findings. *International Journal of the Addictions, 2*(1), 53–84, at 72.

8. *Final report of the Commission of Inquiry into the non-medical use of drugs.* (1973). Ottawa: Information Canada, 310–315.

9. Meissner, C., Recker, S., Reiter, A., Friedrich, H. J., & Oehmichen, M. (2002). Fatal versus non-fatal heroin "overdose": blood morphine concentrations with fatal outcome in comparison to those of intoxicated drivers. *Forensic Science International, 130*(1), 49–54.

10. Darke, S. (2014). Opioid overdose and the power of old myths: What we thought we knew, what we do know and why it matters. *Drug and Alcohol Review, 33*(2), 109–114, at 110.

11. Greene, M. H., Luke, J. L. and Dupont, R. L. (1974). Opiate "overdose" deaths in the District of Columbia I. Heroin-related fatalities. *Medical Annals of the District of Columbia, 43*(4), 175–181, at 175.

12. Cherubin, C., McCusker, J., Baden, M., Kavalier, F., & Amsel, Z. (1972). The epidemiology of death in narcotic addicts. *American Journal of Epidemiology, 96*(1), 11–22, at 11.

13. Werner, A. (1969). Near-fatal hyperacute reaction to intravenously administered heroin. *Journal of the American Medical Association, 207*(12), 2277–2288, at 2277–2278.

14. Darke, Opioid overdose and the power of old myths: What we thought we knew, what we do know and why it matters. 111.

15. Hill, R., Lyndon, A., Withey, S., Roberts, J., Kershaw, Y., MacLachlan, J., Lingford-Hughes, A., Kelly, E., Bailey, C., Hickman, M., & Henderson, G. (2016). Ethanol reversal of tolerance to the respiratory depressant effects of morphine. *Neuropsychopharmacology, 41*(3), 762–773; Mirakbari, S. M. (2004). Heroin overdose as a cause of death:

Truth or myth. *Australian Journal of Forensic Sciences, 36*(2), 73–78; Ruttenber, A. J., Kalter, H. D., & Santinga, P. (1990). The role of ethanol abuse in the etiology of heroin-related death. *Journal of Forensic Sciences, 35*(4), 891–900.

16. White J. M., & Irvine, R. J. (1999). Mechanisms of fatal opioid overdose. *Addiction, 94*(7), 961–972.

17. Fraser, H. F., & Isbell, H. (1952). Comparative effects of 20 mgm. of morphine sulfate on non-addicts and former morphine addicts. *Journal of Pharmacology and Experimental Therapeutics, 105*(4), 498–502.

18. Andrews, H. L. (1943). The effect of opiates on the pain threshold in post-addicts. *Journal of Clinical Investigation, 22*(4), 511–516.

19. Cochin, J., & Kornetsky, C. (1964). Development and loss of tolerance to morphine in the rat after single and multiple injections. *Journal of Pharmacology and Experimental Therapeutics, 145*(1), 1–10; Kayan, S., & Mitchell, C. L. (1972). Studies on tolerance development to morphine: Effect of the dose-interval on the development of single dose tolerance. *Archives Internationales de Pharmacodynamie et de Thérapie, 199*(2), 407–414.

20. Druid, H., Strandberg, J. J., Alkass, K., Nyström, I., Kugelberg, F. C., & Kronstrand, R. (2007). Evaluation of the role of abstinence in heroin overdose deaths using segmental hair analysis. *Forensic Science International, 168*(2–3), 223–226, at 223.

21. Siegel, S., & Ellsworth, D. W. (1986). Pavlovian conditioning and death from apparent overdose of medically prescribed morphine: A case report. *Bulletin of the Psychonomic Society, 24*(4), 278–280.

22. https://www.quora.com/Why-is-it-that-celebrities-seem-to-overdose-only-in-hotels-rather-than-in-their-or-their-friends-houses.

23. Shrira, I., & Aggarwal, Y. (2023). Drug overdose mortality of residents and visitors to cities. *Substance Use & Misuse, 58*(10), 1273–1280.

24. Siegel, S. (1984). Pavlovian conditioning and heroin overdose: Reports by overdose victims. *Bulletin of the Psychonomic Society, 22*(5), 428–430.

25. Siegel, Pavlovian conditioning and heroin overdose, 429.

26. Gutiérrez-Cebollada, J., de la Torre, R., Ortuño, J., Garcés, J., & Camí, J. (1994). Psychotropic drug consumption and other factors associated with heroin overdose. *Drug and Alcohol Dependence, 35*(2), 169–174.

27. Gutiérrez-Cebollada et al., Psychotropic drug consumption, 173.

28. Siegel, S., Hinson, R. E., Krank, M. D., & McCully, J. (1982). Heroin "overdose" death: Contribution of drug-associated environmental cues. *Science, 216*(4544), 436–437.

29. Melchior, C. L. (1990). Conditioned tolerance provides protection against ethanol lethality. *Pharmacology Biochemistry and Behavior, 37*(1), 205–206.

30. Vila, C. J. (1989). Death by pentobarbital overdose mediated by Pavlovian conditioning. *Pharmacology Biochemistry and Behavior, 32*(1), 365–366.

31. Siegel et al., Heroin "overdose" death.

Chapter 4

1. Horrobin, D. F. (1970). *Principles of biological control.* Aylesbury, UK: Medical and Technical Publishing, 1.

2. Bernard, C. (1878/1974). *Lectures on the phenomena of life common to animals and plants* (H. E. Hoff. R. Guillemin, & L. Guillemin, Trans.). Springfield, IL: Charles C. Thomas, 85.

3. Gross, C. G. (1998). Claude Bernard and the constancy of the internal environment. *The Neuroscientist, 4,* 380–385.

4. Cannon, W. B. (1932). *The wisdom of the body.* New York: Norton, 281.

Chapter 5

1. Pavlov, I. P. (1904). *Nobel lecture: Physiology of digestion.* Retrieved November 29, 2013 from http://www.nobelprize.org/nobel_prizes/medicine/laureates/1904/pavlov-lecture.html.

2. Pavlov, *Nobel lecture*.

3. Todes, D. P. (2014). *Ivan Pavlov: A Russian life in science*. New York: Oxford University Press, 516–517.

4. Benjamin, L. T., Jr. (2003). Behavioral science and the Nobel Prize: A history. *American Psychologist, 58*, 731–741.

5. Pavlov, I. P. (1927). *Conditioned reflexes* (G. V. Anrep, Trans.). London: Oxford University Press, 22.

6. Coon, D. J. (1982). Eponymy, obscurity, Twitmeyer, and Pavlov. *Journal of the History of the Behavioral Sciences, 18*, 255–262.

7. Siegel, S., Baptista, M. A. S., Kim, J. A., McDonald, R. V., & Weise-Kelly, L. (2000). Pavlovian psychopharmacology: The associative basis of tolerance. *Experimental and Clinical Psychopharmacology, 8*(3), 276–293.

8. Ramsay, D. S., & Woods, S. C. (1997). Biological consequences of drug administration: Implications for acute and chronic tolerance. *Psychological Review, 104*(1), 170–193; Siegel et al., Pavlovian psychopharmacology.

9. Banaco, R., & Montan, R. (2018). Teoria analítico-comportamental. In N. Zanelatto & R. Laranjeira (Eds.), *O tratamento da dependência química e as terapias cognitivo-comportamentais: Um guia para terapeutas* (2nd ed.), 115–132. Porto Alegre, Brazil: Artmed, at 125. Cited in R. N. M. Montan & R. A. Banaco (2021). Cue exposure therapy for substance use: A complement to functional analysis. In S. M. Oliani, R. A. Reichert, & R. A. Banaco (Eds.), *Behavior analysis and substance dependence: Theory, research and intervention*. Cham, Switzerland: Springer, 89–108, at 96.

10. Carmack, S. A., Keeley, R. J., Vendruscolo, J. C. M., Lowery-Gionta, E. G., Lu, H., Koob, G. F., Stein, E. A., and Vendruscolo, L. F. (2019). Heroin addiction engages negative emotional learning brain circuits in rats. *Journal of Clinical Investigation, 129*(6), 2480–2484, at 2482.

11. Zador, D. (1999). Heroin overdose. New directions for research. *Addiction, 94*(7), 975–976, at 976.

12. Beaton, M. C. (1999). *Death of an addict*. New York: Warner Books, 23.

13. Berridge, V., & Rawson, N. S. B. (1979). Opiate use and legislative control: A nineteenth century case study. *Social Science & Medicine. Part A: Medical Psychology and Medical Sociology, 13A*(3), 351–363.

14. Waldorf, D., Orlick, M., & Reinarman, C. (1974). *Morphine maintenance*. Washington, DC: Drug Abuse Council, 22.

Chapter 6

1. Thomas, R. K. (1997). Correcting some Pavloviana regarding "Pavlov's bell" and Pavlov's "mugging." *American Journal of Psychology, 110*(1), 115–125.

2. Pavlov, I. P. (1957). *Experimental psychology and other essays*. New York: Philosophical Library, 620.

3. Solomon, R. L., & Corbit, J. D. (1974). An opponent-process theory of motivation: I. Temporal dynamics of affect. *Psychological Review, 81*(2), 119–145, at 132.

4. Siegel, S. (1975). Evidence from rats that morphine tolerance is a learned response. *Journal of Comparative and Physiological Psychology, 89*(5), 498–506, at 498.

5. Dworkin, B. R. (1963). *Learning and physiological regulation*. Chicago: University of Chicago Press, 38.

6. Culler, E. A. (1938). Recent advances in some concepts of conditioning. *Psychological Review, 45*, 134–153, at 136.

7. Ramsay, D. S., & Woods, S. C. (2016). Physiological regulation: how it really works. *Cell Metabolism, 24*(3), 361–364, at 362.

8. Dworkin, *Learning and physiological regulation*, 185.

9. Cannon, B. (1994). Walter Bradford Cannon: Reflections on the man and his contributions. *International Journal of Stress Management, 1*(2), 145–158.

Chapter 7

1. Epstein, L. H., Caggiula, A. R., & Stiller, R. (1989). Environment specific tolerance to nicotine. *Psychopharmacology, 97*(2), 235–237; Caggiula, A. R., Epstein, L. H., Antelman, S. M., Saylor, S. S., Perkins, K. A., Knopf, S., & Stiller, R. (1991). Conditioned tolerance to the anorectic and corticosterone-elevating effects of nicotine. *Pharmacology Biochemistry and Behavior, 40*(1), 53–59.

2. Rozin, P., Reff, D., Mark, M., & Schull, J. (1984). Conditioned opponent responses in human tolerance to caffeine. *Bulletin of the Psychonomic Society, 22*, 117–120; Siegel, S., Kim, J. A., & Sokolowska, M. (2003). Situational-specificity of caffeine tolerance. *Circulation, 108*(6), e38.

3. Siegel, S., Baptista, M. A. S., Kim, J. A., McDonald, R. V., & Weise-Kelly, L. (2000). Pavlovian psychopharmacology: The associative basis of tolerance. *Experimental and Clinical Psychopharmacology, 8*, 276–293.

4. Kavaliers, M., & Hirst, M. (1986). Environmental specificity of tolerance to morphine-induced analgesia in a terrestrial snail: generalization of the behavioral model of tolerance. *Pharmacology Biochemistry and Behavior, 25*(6), 1201–1206, at 1201.

5. Farahbakhsh, Z. Z., & Siciliano, C. A. (2023). Pavlovian-conditioned opioid tolerance. *Science Advances, 9*(6), https://www.science.org/doi/10.1126/sciadv.adg6086.

6. Cochin, J., & Kornetsky, C. (1964). Development and loss of tolerance to morphine in the rat after single and multiple injections. *Journal of Pharmacology and Experimental Therapeutics, 145*, 1–10.

7. Epstein, L. H., Caggiula, A. R., Perkins, K. A., McKenzie, S. J., & Smith, J. A. (1991). Conditioned tolerance to the heart rate effects of smoking. *Pharmacology Biochemistry and Behavior, 39*(1), 15–19.

8. Pavlov, I. P. (1927). *Conditioned reflexes* (G. V. Anrep, Trans.). London: Oxford University Press, 48–67.

9. Reviews by Siegel, S. (1999). Drug anticipation and drug addiction: The 1998 H. David Archibald Lecture. *Addiction, 94*, 1113–1124; Siegel et al., Pavlovian psychopharmacology.

10. Kesner, R. P., Priano, D. J., & DeWitt, J. R. (1976). Time-dependent disruption of morphine tolerance by electroconvulsive shock and frontal cortical stimulation. *Science, 194*(4269), 1079–1081, at 1081.

11. Pavlov, *Conditioned reflexes*, 44.

12. Reviewed by Siegel, S., & Ramos, B. M. C. (2002). Applying laboratory research: Drug anticipation and the treatment of drug addiction. *Experimental and Clinical Psychopharmacology, 10*(3), 162–183.

13. Larson, S., & Siegel, S. (1998). Learning and tolerance to the ataxic effect of ethanol. *Pharmacology Biochemistry and Behavior, 61*(1), 131–142, at 141.

14. Siegel, S. (1989). Pharmacological conditioning and drug effects. In A. J. Goudie & M. V. Emmet-Oglesby (Eds.), *Psychoactive drugs: Tolerance and sensitization* (pp.115–180). Clifton, NJ: Humana Press.

15. Carey, B. (2014, February 10). Prescription painkillers seen as a gateway to heroin. *The New York Times*. Retrieved July 24, 2023, from https://www.nytimes.com/2014/02/11/health/prescription-painkillers-seen-as-a-gateway-to-heroin.html#:~:text=But%20for%20some%20patients%2C%20prescription,soothe%20withdrawal%20in%20current%20users

16. Linnoila, M., Stapleton, J. M., Lister, R., Guthrie, S., & Eckhardt, M. (1986). Effects of alcohol on accident risk. *Pathologist, 40*, 36–41.

17. Siegel, S., Hinson, R. E., & Krank, M. D. (1978). The role of pre-drug signals in morphine analgesic tolerance: Support for a Pavlovian conditioning model of tolerance. *Journal of Experimental Psychology: Animal Behavior Processes, 4*(2), 188–196.

18. Siegel, S., Hinson, R. E., & Krank, M. D. (1981). Morphine-induced attenuation of morphine tolerance. *Science, 212*(4502), 1533–1534.

19. Hodgson, R. (1980) Review of *Behavioural tolerance: Research and treatment implications*. *British Journal of Addiction, 75*, 101–102, at 102.

Chapter 8

1. Blum, D. (2023, May 26). Why does day drinking feel different?: A buzz in the sun can hit harder than dinnertime drinks. Experts shed

light on the science. *The New York Times*, 39. Retrieved July 24, 2023, from https://www.nytimes.com/2023/05/26/well/live/day-drinking.html#:~:text=Drinking%20while%20the%20sun%20is,of%20psychiatry%20and%20behavioral%20sciences

2. Jones, B. M. (1974). Circadian variation in the effects of alcohol on cognitive performance. *Quarterly Journal of Studies on Alcohol, 35*(4), 1212–1219, at 1217.

3. González, V. V., Miguez, G., Quezada, V. E., Mallea, J., & Laborda, M. A. (2019). Ethanol tolerance from a Pavlovian perspective. *Psychology & Neuroscience, 12*(4), 495–509.

4. Shapiro, A. P., & Nathan, P. E. (1986). Human tolerance to alcohol: The role of Pavlovian conditioning processes. *Psychopharmacology, 88*(1), 90–95.

5. Birak, K. S., Higgs, S., & Terry, P. (2011). Conditioned tolerance to the effects of alcohol on inhibitory control in humans. *Alcohol and Alcoholism, 46*(6), 686–693.

6. McCusker, C. G., & Brown, K. (1990). Alcohol-predictive cues enhance tolerance to and precipitate "craving" for alcohol in social drinkers. *Journal of Studies on Alcohol, 51*(6), 494–499.

7. Remington, B., Roberts, P., & Glautier, S. (1997). The effects of drink familiarity on tolerance to alcohol. *Addictive Behaviors, 22*(1), 45–53.

8. Birak, K. S., Terry, P., & Higgs, S. (2010). Effect of cues associated with an alcoholic beverage on executive function. *Journal of Studies on Alcohol and Drugs, 71*(4), 562–569, at 569.

9. United States Food and Drug Administration (2010, November 17). Warning letter. Retreived July 24, 2023, from https://www.ftc.gov/sites/default/files/documents/public_statements/potentially-illegal-marketing-caffeinated-alcohol-products/phusionletter.pdf

10. Siegel, S. (2011). The four-loko effect. *Perspectives on Psychological Science, 6*(4), 357–362; Verster, J. C., Aufricht, C., & Alford, C. (2012). Energy drinks mixed with alcohol: misconceptions, myths, and facts. *International Journal of General Medicine, 5*, 187–198.

11. Bruni, F. (2010, October 31). Caffeine and alcohol: Wham! bam! boozled. *The New York Times*, WK5. Retrieved December 17, 2013, from www.nytimes.com/2010/10/31/weekinreview/31bruni.html

12. Bruni, Caffeine and alcohol.

13. Brooks, D. C., Karamanlian, B. R., & Foster, V. L. (2001). Extinction and spontaneous recovery of ataxic tolerance to ethanol in rats. *Psychopharmacology, 153*(4), 491–496; Crowell, C. R., Hinson, R. E., & Siegel, S. (1981). The role of conditional drug responses in tolerance to the hypothermic effects of ethanol. *Psychopharmacology, 73*(1), 51–54; Duncan, P. M., Alici, T., & Woodward, J. D. (2000). Conditioned compensatory response to ethanol as indicated by locomotor activity in rats. *Behavioural Pharmacology, 11*(5), 395–402; Mansfield, J. G., & Cunningham, C. L. (1980). Conditioning and extinction of tolerance to the hypothermic effect of ethanol in rats. *Journal of Comparative and Physiological Psychology, 94*(5), 962–976; Tiffany, S. T., McCal, K. J., & Maude-Griffin, P. M. (1987). The contribution of classical conditioning to tolerance to the antinociceptive effects of ethanol. *Psychopharmacology, 92*(4), 524–528.

14. Miler, K., Kuszewska, K., Privalova, V., & Woyciechowski, M. (2018). Honeybees show adaptive reactions to ethanol exposure. *Scientific Reports, 8*(1), 1–6.

15. Cappell, H., Roach, C., & Poulos, C. X. (1981). Pavlovian control of cross-tolerance between pentobarbital and ethanol. *Psychopharmacology, 74*(1), 54–57.

16. Ruiz-García, R. I., Cedillo, L. N., Jiménez, J. C., & Miranda, F. (2022). Role of drug-associated environmental stimuli in the development of cross-tolerance to the tachycardic effects of nicotine and alcohol in humans. *Adicciones, 34*(1), 51–59.

Chapter 9

1. Rush, B. (1805). *Medical inquiries and observations* (Vol. 1). Philadelphia: J. Conrad and Company, 380.

2. Bronstein, A. M., Bunday, K. L., & Reynolds, R. (2009). What the "broken escalator" phenomenon teaches us about balance. *Annals of the New York Academy of Sciences, 1164,* 82–88.

3. Lancaster, B. (1995) *The department store: A social history.* London: Leicester University Press, 50.

4. Bolkenius, M. (1970). Escalator injuries in children. *Deutsche Mediziniche Wochenschrift, 95*(7), 321–323.

5. https://www.facebook.com/The-Little-Rascals-152928631442325/videos/the-little-rascals-mike-fright/2691605197516515/

6. Pangborn, R. M. (1968). Parotid flow stimulated by the sight, feel, atend odor of lemon. *Perceptual and Motor Skills, 27*(3), 1340–1342; Christensen, C. M., & Naazesh, M. (1984). Anticipatory salivary flow to the sight of different foods. *Appetite, 5*(4), 307–315; Corty E. W, & Coon, B. (1995). The extinction of naturally occurring conditioned reactions in psychoactive substance users: Analog studies. *Addictive Behaviors, 20*(5), 605–618.

7. Falls, W. A., & Kelsey, J. E. (1989). Procedures that produce context-specific tolerance to morphine in rats also produce context-specific withdrawal. *Behavioral Neuroscience, 103*(4), 842–849.

8. Poulos, C. X., & Cappell, H. (1991). Homeostatic theory of drug tolerance: A general model of physiological adaption. *Psychological Review, 98*(3), 390–426, at 402.

9. Siegel, S. (1991). Feedforward processes in drug tolerance. In R. G. Lister & H. J. Weingartner (Eds.), *Perspectives in cognitive neuroscience* (pp. 405–416). New York: Oxford University Press, at 412.

10. See reviews: Carter, B. L., & Tiffany, S. T. (1999). Meta-analysis of cue-reactivity in addiction research. *Addiction, 94*(3), 327–340; Childress, A. R., McLellan, A. T., & O'Brien, C. P. (1986). Conditioned responses in a methadone population: A comparison of laboratory, clinic, and natural settings. *Journal of Substance Abuse Treatment, 3*(3), 173–179; Siegel, S. (1999). Drug anticipation and drug addiction: The H. David Archibald Lecture, *Addiction, 94*(8), 1113–1124; Siegel, S., &

Ramos, B. C. (2002). Applying laboratory research: Drug anticipation and the treatment of drug addiction. *Experimental and Clinical Psychopharmacology, 10*(3), 162–183.

11. Shephard, A. & Barrett, S. P. (2022). The impacts of caffeine administration, expectancies, and related stimuli on coffee craving, withdrawal, and self-administration. *Journal of Pharmacology, 36*(3), 378–386.

12. Ternes, J. W. (1977). An opponent process theory of habitual behavior with special reference to smoking. In M. E. Jarvik, J. W. Cullen, E. R. Gritz, T. M. Vogt, & L. J. West (Eds.), *Research on smoking behavior* (pp. 157–182). National Institute on Drug Abuse Research Monograph 17. DHEW Pub. No. (ADM) 78–581. Washington, DC: Superintendent of Documents, U.S. Government Printing Office.

13. For a review see, Siegel, Drug anticipation and drug addiction.

14. Imeh-Nathaniel, A., Okon, M., Huber, R., & Nathaniel, T. I. (2014). Exploratory behavior and withdrawal signs in Crayfish: Chronic central morphine injections and termination effects. *Behavioural Brain Research, 264*, 181–187.

15. O'Brien, C. P. (1976). Experimental analysis of conditioning factors in human narcotic addiction. *Pharmacological Review, 27*(4), 533–543, at 533.

16. Kissin, B. (1983). The disease concept of alcoholism. In R. G. Smart, F. B. Glaser, Y. Israel, H. Kalant, R. E. Popham, & W. Schmidt, *Research advances in alcohol and drug problems* (Vol. 7, pp. 93–126). New York: Plenum, 113.

17. Mussulman, L. M., Scheuermann, T. S., Faseru, B., Nazir, N., & Richter, K. P. (2019). Rapid relapse to smoking following hospital discharge. *Preventive Medicine Reports, 15*, 1–4.

18. Teasdale, J. D. (1973). Conditioned abstinence in narcotic addicts. *International Journal of the Addictions, 8*(2), 273–292.

19. Trujillo, H. M., Oviedo-Joekes, E., and Vargas, C. (2005). Anticipatory conditioned responses to subjective and physiological effects of

heroin in addicted persons. *International Journal of Clinical and Health Psychology*, 5(3), 423–443.

20. Wikler, A. (1977). The search for the psyche in drug dependence: A 35-year retrospective survey, *Journal of Nervous and Mental Disease*, 165(1), 29–40.

21. Biernacki, P. (1988). *Pathways from heroin addiction: Recovery without treatment.* Philadelphia: Temple University Press, 1988, 108.

22. Biernacki, *Pathways from heroin addiction*, 115.

23. Teasdale, Conditioned abstinence in narcotic addicts.

24. Biernacki, *Pathways from heroin addiction*, 109.

25. Childress, A.R., Ehrman, R., Rohsenow, D.J., Robbins, S.J. & O'Brien, C. (1992). Classically conditioned factors in drug dependence. In J. Lowinson, P. Ruiz, R. Millman, & J. Langrod (Eds.), *Substance abuse: A comprehensive textbook* (pp. 56–69). Baltimore: Williams and Wilkins, 56.

26. Wikler, The search for the psyche in drug dependence, 35.

27. Macnish, R. (1835). *The anatomy of drunkenness.* New York: D. Appleton and Co., 158.

28. Macnish, *The anatomy of drunkenness*, 167–168.

29. Macnish, *The anatomy of drunkenness*, 168.

Chapter 10

1. Anonymous (2001). *Alcoholics Anonymous: The story of how many thousands of men and women have recovered from alcoholism* (4th ed.). New York: Alcoholics Anonymous World Services.

2. Schasre, R. (1966). Cessation patterns among neophyte heroin users. *International Journal of the Addictions*, 1(2), 23–32, at 28–29.

3. Ross, S. (1973). A study of living and residence patterns of former heroin addicts as a result of their participation in a methadone treatment program. In *Proceedings of the Fifth National Conference on*

Methadone Treatment (pp. 554–561). New York: National Association for the Prevention of Addiction to Narcotics, 561.

4. Frykholm, B. (1979). Termination of the drug career: An interview study of 58 ex-addicts. *Acta Psychiatrica Scandinavica, 59*(4), 370–380, at 376.

5. Kirk, D. S. (2019). The association between residential relocation and re-incarceration among drug-dependent former prisoners. *Addiction, 114*(8), 1389–1395, at 1389.

6. Snoek, A., Levy, N., & Kennett, J. (2016). Strong-willed but not successful: The importance of strategies in recovery from addiction. *Addictive Behaviors Reports, 4*, 102–107, at 106.

7. Rachlis, B. S., Wood, E., Li, K., Hogg, R. S., & Kerr, T. (2010). Drug and HIV-related risk behaviors after geographic migration among a cohort of injection drug users. *AIDS and Behavior, 14*(4), 854–861.

8. Genberg, B. L., Gange, S. J., Go, V. F., Celentano, D. D., Kirk, G. D., Latkin, C. A., & Mehta, S. H. (2011). The effect of neighborhood deprivation and residential relocation on long-term injection cessation among injection drug users (IDUs) in Baltimore, Maryland. *Addiction, 106*(11), 1966–1974.

9. Cooper, H. L., Bonney, L. E., Ross, Z., Karnes, C., Hunter-Jones, J., Kelley, M. E., & Rothenberg, R. (2013). The aftermath of public housing relocation: Relationship to substance misuse. *Drug and Alcohol Dependence, 133*(1), 37–44.

10. Bammer, G., & Weekes, S. (1994). Becoming an ex-user: insights into the process and implications for treatment and policy. *Drug and Alcohol Review, 13*(3), 285–292.

11. Maddux, J. F., & Desmond, D. P. (1982). Residence relocation inhibits opioid dependence. *Archives of General Psychiatry, 39*(11), 1313–1317.

12. Richard Nixon, Special message to the Congress on control of narcotics and dangerous drugs, July 14, 1969. http://www.presidency.ucsb.edu/ws/index.php?pid=2126&st=&st1=

13. Helzer, J. E. (2010). Significance of the Robins et al. Vietnam veterans study. *American Journal on Addiction, 19*(3), 218–221, at 218.

14. Published in the *New York Times*, May 28, 1971.

15. *Time*, June 8, 1971, quoted in Baum, D. (1996). *Smoke and mirrors: The war on drugs and the politics of failure*. Boston: Little, Brown.

16. Richard Nixon, Special message to the Congress on drug abuse prevention and control, June 17, 1971. http://www.presidency.ucsb.edu/ws/?pid=3048

17. Senate testimony (1972). Hearing before the Subcommittee to Investigate Juvenile Delinquency of the Committee on the Judiciary United States Senate, Ninety Second Congress, U.S. Government Printing Office, Washington, DC, 481.

18. The history of the Nixon administration's dealings with the Vietnam soldiers' heroin addiction problems has been summarized in Baum, *Smoke and mirrors*, chapter 3, "Pee House of the August Moon, 1971"; and in Massing, M. (1998). *The fix*. Berkeley, CA: University of California Press.

19. Massing, *The fix*, 110.

20. Jaffe, J. H. (2010). A follow-up of Vietnam drug users: Origins and context of Lee Robins' classic study. *American Journal on Addictions, 19*(3), 212–214, at 212.

21. Massing, *The fix*, 114.

22. Robins, L. N., Davis, D. H., & Nurco, D. N. (1974). How permanent was Vietnam drug addiction? *American Journal of Public Health Supplement, 64*, 38–43, at 38.

23. Robins, L. N.; Helzer, J. E., & Davis, D. H. (1975) Narcotic use in Southeast Asia and afterwards. *Archives of General Psychiatry, 32*, 955–961.

24. Robins et al. Narcotic use in Southeast Asia and afterwards, 958.

25. O'Brien, C. P., Nace, E. P., Mintz, J., Meyers, A. L., & Ream, N. (1980). Follow-up of Vietnam veterans. I. Relapse to drug use after Vietnam service. *Drug and Alcohol Dependence, 5*(5), 333–340.

26. Robins, L. N. (1993). Vietnam veterans' rapid recovery from heroin addiction: A fluke or normal expectation? *Addiction, 88,* 1041–1054, at 1041.

27. Thompson, T., & Ostlund Jr, W. (1965). Susceptibility to readdiction as a function of the addiction and withdrawal environments. *Journal of Comparative and Physiological Psychology, 60*(3), 388–392.

28. Hinson, R. E., Poulos, C. X., Thomas, W., & Cappell, H. (1986). Pavlovian conditioning and addictive behavior: Relapse to oral self administration of morphine. *Behavioral Neuroscience, 100*(3), 368–375.

Chapter 11

1. Mello, N. K., & Mendelson, J. H. (1970). Experimentally induced intoxication in alcoholics: A comparison between programed and spontaneous drinking. *Journal of Pharmacology and Experimental Therapeutics, 173*(1), 101–116, at 111.

2. Johanson, C. E., & Schuster, C. R. (1981). Animal models of drug self-administration. In N. Mello (Ed.), *Advances in substance abuse* (Vol. 2, pp. 219–297). Greenwich, CT: JAI Press, 280.

3. Siegel, S., Hinson, R. E., & Krank, M. D. (1978). The role of predrug signals in morphine analgesic tolerance: Support for a Pavlovian conditioning model of tolerance. *Journal of Experimental Psychology: Animal Behavior Processes, 4*(2), 188–196.

4. Eliot, T. S. (1932). *Selected essays, 1917–1932.* New York: Harcourt Brace, at 377.

5. Collins, W. (1868/1966). *The moonstone.* London: Harmondsworth, 465.

6. Actually, *The Moonstone* contains many insights into drug effects that were not established by the scientific community until well into the twentieth century. For summaries, see Siegel, S. (1983). Wilkie

Collins: Victorian novelist as psychopharmacologist. *Journal of the History of Medicine and Allied Sciences, 38*(2), 161–175; Siegel, S. (1985). Psychopharmacology and the mystery of *The Moonstone*. *American Psychologist, 40*(5), 580–581; Siegel, S. (1982). Drug dissociation in the nineteenth century. In F. C. Colpaert & J. L. Slangen (Eds.), *Drug discrimination: Applications in CNS pharmacology* (pp. 257–261). Amsterdam: Elsevier/North Holland Biomedical Press.

7. Davis, N. P. (1956). *The life of Wilkie Collins*. Urbana, IL: University of Illinois Press, 255.

8. Hayter, A. (1970). *Opium and the romantic imagination*. Berkeley, CA: University of California Press; Robinson, K. (1951). *Wilkie Collins: A biography*. New York: Macmillan, 214; Siegel, Wilkie Collins: Victorian novelist as psychopharmacologist.

9. Corti, R., Binggeli, C., Sudano, I., Spieker, L., Hänseler, E., Ruschitzka, F., Chaplin, W. F., Lüscher, T. F., & Noll, G. (2002). Coffee acutely increases sympathetic nerve activity and blood pressure independently of caffeine content: Role of habitual versus nonhabitual drinking. *Circulation, 106*(23), 2935–2940.

10. Siegel, S., Sokolowska, M., & Kim, J. A. (2003). Caffeine and coffee tolerance. *Circulation, 108*(6), e38.

11. Ehrman, R., Ternes, J., O'Brien, C. P., & McLellan, A. T. (1992). Conditioned tolerance in human opiate addicts. *Psychopharmacology, 108*(1), 218–224, at 218.

12. Lovallo, W. R., Whitsett, T. L., & Wilson, M. F. (2003) Caffeine and coffee tolerance. *Circulation, 108*(6), e38-e39; Corti, R., Binggeli, C., Sudano, I., Spieker, L., Ruschitzka, F., Lüscher, T. F., Noll, G., Hänseler, E., & Chaplin, W. F. (2003). Caffeine and coffee tolerance. *Circulation, 108*(6), e40.

13. For reviews, see MacRae, J. R., & Siegel, S. (1997). The role of self-administration in morphine withdrawal in rats. *Psychobiology, 25*(1), 77–82; Weise-Kelly, L., & Siegel, S. (2001). Self-administration cues as signals: Drug self-administration and tolerance. *Journal of Experimental Psychology: Animal Behavior Processes, 27*(2), 125–136.

14. Twining, R. C., Bolan, M., & Grigson, P. S. (2009). Yoked delivery of cocaine is aversive and protects against the motivation for the drug in rats. *Behavioral Neuroscience, 123*(4), 913–925.

Chapter 12

1. Meyer, R. E., & Mirin, S. M. (1979). *The heroin stimulus: Implications for a theory of addiction*. New York: Plenum Press.

2. Schoenmakers, T., Wiers, R. W., & Field, M. (2008). Effects of a low dose of alcohol on cognitive biases and craving in heavy drinkers. *Psychopharmacology, 197*(1), 169–178.

3. Bigelow, G. E., Griffiths, R. R., & Liebson, I. A. (1977). Pharmacological influences upon human ethanol self-administration. In M. M. Gross (Ed.), *Alcohol intoxication and withdrawal* (pp. 523–538). New York: Plenum Press; Hodgson, R., Rankin, H., & Stockwell, T. (1979). Alcohol dependence and the priming effect. *Behavior Research and Therapy, 17*(4), 379–387; Ludwig, A. M., & Wikler, A. (1974). "Craving" and relapse to drink. *Quarterly Journal of Studies on Alcohol, 35*(1), 108–130; Goddard, M. J. (1999). The role of US signal value in contingency, drug conditioning, and learned helplessness. *Psychonomic Bulletin and Review, 6*(3), 412–423; Ludwig, A. M., & Stark, L. H. (1974). Alcohol craving: Subjective and situational aspects. *Quarterly Journal of Studies on Alcohol, 35*(3), 899–905; Siegel, S. (1987). Pavlovian conditioning and ethanol tolerance. In K. O. Lindros, R. Ylikahri, & K. Kiianmaa (Eds.), *Advances in biomedical alcohol research* (pp. 25–36). Oxford: Pergamon Press.

4. Schacter, S., Silverstein, B., Kozlowski, L. T., Perlick, D., Herman, C. P., & Liebling, B. (1977). Studies of the interaction of psychological and pharmacological determinants of smoking: 1. Nicotine regulation in heavy and light smokers. *Journal of Experimental Psychology: General, 106*(1), 5–12.

5. de Wit, H. (1996). Priming effects with drugs and other reinforcers. *Experimental and Clinical Psychopharmacology, 4*(1), 5–10; McDonald, R. V., & Siegel, S. (2004). Intra-administration associations and

withdrawal symptoms: Morphine-elicited morphine withdrawal. *Experimental and Clinical Psychopharmacology, 12*(1), 3–11.

6. Goudie, A. J. (1990). Conditioned opponent processes in the development of tolerance to psychoactive drugs. *Progress in Neuro-Psychopharmacology & Biological Psychiatry, 14*(5), 675–688, at 679.

7. Greeley, J., Lê, D. A., Poulos, C. X., & Cappell, H. (1984). Alcohol is an effective cue in the conditional control of tolerance to alcohol. *Psychopharmacology, 83*(2), 159–162.

8. McDonald & Siegel, Intra-administration associations and withdrawal symptoms; Krank, M. D. (1987). Conditioned hyperalgesia depends on the pain sensitivity measure. *Behavioral Neuroscience, 101*(6), 854–857; Sokolowska, M., Siegel, S., & Kim, J. A. (2002). Intra-administration associations: Conditional hyperalgesia elicited by morphine onset cues. *Journal of Experimental Psychology: Animal Behavior Processes, 28*(3), 309–320; Cepeda-Benito, A., & Short, P. (2008). Morphine's interoceptive stimuli as cues for the development of associative morphine tolerance in the rat. *Psychobiology, 25*(3), 236–240.

9. Kim, J. A., Siegel, S. & Patenall, V. R. A. (1999). Drug-onset cues as signals: Intra-administration associations and tolerance. *Journal of Experimental Psychology: Animal Behavior Processes, 25*(4), 491–504; McDonald & Siegel, Intra-administration associations and withdrawal symptoms; Sokolowska, Siegel, & Kim, Intra-administration associations.

10. Goddard, The role of US signal value in contingency, drug conditioning, and learned helplessness, 418.

11. de Wit, Priming effects with drugs and other reinforcers, 5.

Chapter 13

1. Bradley, P. B., & Moorey, S. (1988). Extinction of craving during exposure to drug-related cues: Three single case reports. *Behavioral Psychotherapy, 16*(1), 45–56.

2. Weinstein, A., Lingford-Hughes, A., Martinez-Raga, J., & Marshall, J. (1998). What makes alcohol-dependent individuals early in

abstinence crave for alcohol: Exposure to the drink, images of drinking, or remembrance of drinks past? *Alcohol Clinical and Experimental Research, 22*(6), 1376–1381.

3. Drobes, D. J., & Tiffany, S. T. (1997). Induction of smoking urge through imaginal and in vivo procedures: Physiological and self-report manifestations. *Journal of Abnormal Psychology, 106*(1), 15–25.

4. Ludwig, A. M., & Stark, L. H. (1974). Alcohol craving: Subjective and situational aspects. *Quarterly Journal of Studies on Alcohol, 35*(3), 899–905.

5. Mathew, R. J., Claghorn, J. L., & Largen, J. (1979). Craving for alcohol in sober alcoholics. *American Journal of Psychiatry, 136*(4B): 603–606, at 605.

6. Greeley, J., & Ryan, C. (1995). The role of interoceptive cues for drug delivery in conditioning models of drug dependence. In D. C. Drummond, S. T. Tiffany, S. Glautier, & B. Remington (Eds.), *Addictive behaviour: Cue exposure theory and practice* (pp. 121–136). New York: Wiley; Epstein, D. H., Willner-Reid, J., Vahabzadch, M., Mezghanni, M., Lin, J.-L., & Prestin, K. L. (2009). Real-time electronic diary reports of cue exposure and mood in the hours before cocaine and heroin craving and use. *Archives of General Psychiatry, 66*(1), 88–94.

7. Poulos, C. X., Hinson, R. E., & Siegel, S. (1981). The role of Pavlovian processes in drug tolerance and dependence: Implications for treatment. *Addictive Behaviors, 6*(3), 205–211, at 209.

8. O'Brien, C. P. (1976). Experimental analysis of conditioning factors in human narcotic addiction. *Pharmacological Reviews, 27*(4), 533–543, at 534.

Chapter 14

1. Corty, E. W, & Coon, B. (1995). The extinction of naturally occurring conditioned reactions in psychoactive substance users: Analog studies. *Addictive Behaviors, 20*(5), 605–618.

2. Chiauzzi, E. J., & Lilegren, S. (1993). Taboo topics in addiction treatment: An empirical review of clinical folklore. *Journal of Substance Abuse Treatment, 10*(3), 303–316, at 309.

3. Drummond, D. C., Tiffany, S. T., Glautier, S., & Remington, B. (Eds.). (1995). *Addictive behaviour: Cue exposure theory and practice*. New York: John Wiley & Sons.

4. For reviews of cue exposure, see Siegel, S. & Ramos, B. C. (2002). Applying laboratory research: Drug anticipation and the treatment of drug addiction. *Experimental and Clinical Psychopharmacology, 10*(3), 162–183; Marissen, M. A. E., Franken, I. H. A., Blanken, P., Van Den Brink, W, & Hendricks, V. M. (2005). Cue exposure therapy for opiate dependent clients. *Journal of Substance Use, 10*(2–3): 97–105, https://doi.org/10.1080/1465980512331344075; Martin, T., LaRowe, S. D., & Malcolm, R. (2010). Progress in cue exposure therapy for the treatment of addictive disorders: A review update. *Open Addiction Journal, 3*, 92–101.

5. Carroll, K. M. (1999). Behavioral and cognitive behavioral treatments. In B. McCrady & E. S. Epstein (Eds.), *Addictions: A comprehensive guidebook* (pp. 250–267). New York: Oxford, University Press, 261.

6. Tobeña, A., Fernández-Teruel, A., Escorihuela, R. M., Núñez, J. F., Zapata, A., Ferré, P., & Sánchez, R. (1993). Limits of habituation and extinction: Implications for relapse prevention programs in addictions. *Drug and Alcohol Dependence, 32*(3), 209–217, at 215.

7. Cepeda-Benito, A., & Short, P. (1997). Morphine's interoceptive stimuli as cues for the development of associative morphine tolerance in the rat. *Psychobiology, 25*(3), 236–240, at 239.

8. Sitharthan, T., Sitharthan, G., Hough, M. J., & Kavanagh, D. J. (1997). Cue exposure in moderation drinking: A comparison with cognitive–behavior therapy. *Journal of Consulting and Clinical Psychology, 65*(5), 878–882.

9. Sitharthan, T., Sitharthan, G., & Kavanagh, D. J. (2001). Emotional cue exposure for alcohol abuse: Development of a new treatment procedure to train moderation drinking in the context of dysphoria. *Clinical Psychology and Psychotherapy, 8*(1), 73–78.

10. Otto, M. W, O'Cleirigh, C. M., & Pollack, M. H. (2007). Attending to emotional cues for drug abuse: Bridging the gap between clinic and home behaviors. *Psychological and Brain Sciences, 3*(2), 48–55.

11. Pavlov, I. P. (1927). *Conditioned reflexes* (G. V. Anrep, Trans.). London: Oxford University Press, 58.

12. Hammersley, R. (1992). Cue exposure and learning theory. *Addictive Behaviors, 17*(3), 297–300.

13. For example, Corty & Coon, The extinction of naturally occurring conditioned reactions.

14. Mackintosh, N. J. (1974). *The psychology of animal learning*. London: Academic Press, 421–422.

15. Bouton, M. E. (2000). A learning theory perspective on lapse, relapse, and the maintenance of behavior change. *Health Psychology, 19*(1), 57–63, at 57.

16. Zironi, I., Burattini, C., Aicardi, G., & Janak, P. H. (2006). Context is a trigger for relapse to alcohol. *Behavioural Brain Research, 167*(1), 150–155.

17. Blakey, R., & Baker, R. (1980). An exposure approach to alcohol abuse. *Behavior Research and Therapy, 18*(4), 319–325.

18. Sayette, M. A., & Goodwin, M. E. (2020). Augmented reality in addiction: Promises and challenges. *Clinical Psychology: Science and Practice, 27*(3), e12366; Vinci, C., Brandon, K. O., Kleinjan, M., & Brandon, T. H. (2020). The clinical potential of augmented reality. *Clinical Psychology: Science and Practice, 27*(3), e12357.

19. Strang, J., McCambridge, J., Best, D., Beswick, T., Bearn, J., Rees, S., & Gossop, M. (2003). Loss of tolerance and overdose mortality after inpatient opiate detoxification: Follow up study. *BMJ, 326*(7396), 959–960.

Chapter 15

1. Jha, P. (2020). The hazards of smoking and the benefits of cessation: A critical summation of the epidemiological evidence in high-income countries. *eLife, 9,* e49979, https://elifesciences.org/articles/49979#x9d97bad3

2. Arntzen, F. I. (1948). Some psychological aspects of nicotinism. *American Journal of Psychology, 61*(3), 424–425, at 425.

3. Kandel, D. B., & Chen, K. (2000) Extent of smoking and nicotine dependence in the United States: 1991–1993. *Nicotine & Tobacco Research, 2*(3), 263–274.

4. Russell, M. A., & Feyerabend, C. (1978). Cigarette smoking: A dependence on high-nicotine boli, *Drug Metabolism Reviews, 8*(1), 29–57, at 30–31.

5. Babb, S., Malarcher, A., Schauer, G., Asman, K. & Jamal, A. (2017). Quitting smoking among adults—United States, 2000–2015. *Morbidity and Mortality Weekly Report, 65*(52), 1457–1464.

6. Heishman, S. J., Kleykamp, B. A., & Singleton, E. G. (2010). Meta-analysis of the acute effects of nicotine and smoking on human performance. *Psychopharmacology, 210*(4), 453–469

Chapter 16

1. Zinberg, N. E. (1984). *Drug, set, and setting: The basis for controlled intoxicant use.* New Haven, CT: Yale University Press.

2. Harding, G., (1988). Patterns of heroin use: What do we know? *British Journal of Addiction, 83(11), 1247*–1254.

3. Ritchie, H., & Roser, M. (2018). Alcohol consumption. Published online at OurWorldInData.org. Retrieved from https://ourworldindata.org/alcohol-consumption

4. Collins, W. (1977). *Armadale.* New York: Dover Press, 376–377. (Original work published serially in *The Cornhill Magazine,* November 1864–June 1866)

5. Hart, C. L. (2021). *Drug use for grown-ups: Chasing liberty in the land of fear.* New York: Penguin Press.

6. Schuckit, M. A. (1994). A low level of response to alcohol as a predictor of future alcoholism. *American Journal of Psychiatry, 151*(2), 184–189, at 184.

7. McBride, W. J., & Li, T. K. (1998). Animal models of alcoholism: Neurobiology of high alcohol-drinking behavior in rodents. *Critical Reviews in Neurobiology, 12*(4), 339–369.

8. Nishida, K. S., Park, T. Y., Lee, B. H., Ursano, R. J., & Choi, K. H. (2016). Individual differences in initial morphine sensitivity as a predictor for the development of opiate addiction in rats. *Behavioural Brain Research, 313*, 315–323.

9. Ramsay, D. S., & Woods, S. C. (1997). Biological consequences of drug administration: Implications for acute and chronic tolerance, *Psychological Review, 104*(1), 170–193; Ramsay, D. S., Kiyala, K. J., & Woods, S. C. (2014). Correctly identifying responses is critical for understanding homeostatic and allostatic regulation, *Temperature, 1*(3), 157–159; Ramsay, D. S., Kiyala, K. J., & Woods, S. C. (2020). Individual differences in biological regulation: Predicting vulnerability to drug addiction, obesity, and other dysregulatory disorders. *Experimental and Clinical Psychopharmacology, 28*(4), 388–403.

10. Cofresí, R. U., Kohen, C. B., Motschman, C. A., Wiers, R. W., Piaseci, T. M., & Bartholow, B. D. (2022). Behavioral response bias and event-related brain potentials implicate elevated incentive salience attribution to alcohol cues in emerging adults with lower sensitivity to alcohol. *Addiction, 117*(4), 892–904; Fleming, K. A., & Bartholow, B. D. (2014). Alcohol cues, approach bias, and inhibitory control: Applying a dual process model of addiction to alcohol sensitivity. *Psychology of Addictive Behaviors, 28*(1), 85–96; Fleming, K. A., Cofresí, R. U., & Bartholow, B. D. (2021). Transfer of incentive salience from a first-order alcohol cue to a novel second-order alcohol cue among individuals at risk for alcohol use disorder: Electrophysiological evidence. *Addiction, 116*(7), 1734–1746; Kohen, C. B., Cofresí, R. U., Bartholow, B. D., & Piasecki, T. M. (2023). Alcohol craving in the natural environment: Moderating roles of cue exposure, drinking, and alcohol sensitivity. *Experimental and Clinical Psychopharmacology, 31*(1), 57–71.

11. Agar, M. (1973). *Ripping and running: A formal ethnography of urban heroin addicts.* New York: Seminar Press.

Chapter 17

1. Leshner, A. I. (1997). Addiction is a brain disease, and it matters. *Science, 278*(5335), 45–47, at 46.

2. Levy, N. (2013). Addiction is not a brain disease (and it matters). *Frontiers in Psychiatry, 4*: 1–7, https://www.frontiersin.org/articles/10.3389/fpsyt.2013.00024/full

3. Lewis, M. (2018). Brain change in addiction as learning, not disease. *New England Journal of Medicine, 379*(16): 1551–1560.

4. Ersche, K. D., Williams, G. B., Robbins, T. W., & Bullmore, E. T. (2013). Meta-analysis of structural brain abnormalities associated with stimulant drug dependence and neuroimaging of addiction vulnerability and resilience. *Current Opinion in Neurobiology, 23*(4), 615–624.

5. Hall, W., Carter, A., & Forlini, C. (2015). The brain disease model of addiction: is it supported by the evidence and has it delivered on its promises? *The Lancet Psychiatry, 2*(1), 105–110.

6. Grifell, M., & Hart, C. L. (2018). Is drug addiction a brain disease? *American Scientist, 106*(3), 160–167.

7. Satel, S., & Lilenfield, S. O. (2013). *Brainwashed: The seductive appeal of mindless neuroscience*. New York: Basic Books, 56–57.

8. Winick, C. (1962). Maturing out of narcotic addiction. *Bulletin on Narcotics, 14*(1), 1–7; Heyman, G. M. (2009). *Addiction: A disorder of choice*. Cambridge, MA: Harvard University Press.

9. Heim, D. (2014). Addiction: Not just brain malfunction. *Nature, 507*(7490), 40.

10. Salaverria, L. (2017, May 10). Duterte insists shabu can cause brain damage. *Philippine Daily Inquirer*. Retrieved from newsinfo.inquirer.net/895885/Duterte-insists-shabu-can-cause-brain-damage

11. Ma, S., Zhang, C., Yuan, T. F., Steele, D., Voon, V., & Sun, B. (2020). Neurosurgical treatment for addiction: lessons from an untold

story in China and a path forward. *National Science Review, 7*(3), 702–712.

Chapter 18

1. Langley, L. L. (Ed.). (1973). *Homeostasis: Origins of a concept.* Stroudsburg, PA: Dowden, Hutchison and Ross, 293.

Index

Alcohol, 57–66
  abuse and cue-exposure therapy, 119, 121–124
  in colonial America, 3–4
  and conditional homeostatic response, 37
  craving in drinking environment, 4, 78–79
  craving and relapse elicited by negative emotional stimuli, 114
  and environmental specificity of tolerance, 50
  and learned tolerance, 56
  has lethal effect if high dose given in novel environment, 22
  versus morphine, 6
  self-administration vs. coerced consumption, 96–100
  susceptibility to addiction, 132–135
  and use with heroin, 15
Alcoholics Anonymous, 82, 110
Arntzen, F. I., 128–129

Barcelona, case study in, 20, 21, 39
Bernard, Claude, 26–27, 29, 143
Biernacki, Patrick, 2, 75–76
Black, J. R., 6
Bouton, Mark, 123
Brecher, Edward, 12
Brain disease view of addiction, 138–139
  evidence contrary to, 140–141
  untoward effects of, 141–142
Brown, Kia, 60–61
Bruni, Frank, 63–64

Caffeine, 37, 50, 62–63, 67, 103–105
Cannon, Walter B., 27, 29, 41, 43–47, 143
Cappell, Harold, 71–72
Carroll, Kathleen M., 120
Cherubin, Charles, 15
Chesney, Marion (M. C. Beaton), 40

Index

Cigarettes. *See* Nicotine and smoking
Collins, Wilkie, 101–103, 132
Conditional response. *See also* Pavlovian conditioning
  based on drugs, 37–40, 45–46, 49–53, 72, 107–109, 119–120, 129, 138, 144
  elimination of (extinction), 52–53, 118–124
  external inhibition of, 53–55
  formation of, 34
  as the ghost that haunts the addict, 38–39, 50, 73, 76, 82, 93, 115, 117, 119, 138, 142, 145
  occurring when it's unwanted, 67ff
Corbit, John, 44–45
Cross tolerance, 66
Cue exposure as an addiction treatment
  improving effectiveness of, 120–125
  ineffectiveness of, 119–120
Culler, Elmer, 46–47

Darke, Shane, 12, 14, 15
De Wit, Harriet, 110–111
Drug legislation
  before legislation prohibiting any drugs, 5–6
  following legislation prohibiting some drugs, 6–7
Drug preparation. *See* "Withdrawal symptoms" as drug preparation symptoms

Duterte, Rodrigo, 141–142
Dworkin, Barry R., 46, 47, 143

E. C., case study, 54
Ehrman, Ronald, 104
Epstein, Leonard, 51–52

Four Loko, 62–65

Gerevich, József, 12, 17
  and K. J. case study, 12–14, 16, 17
Goddard, Murray, 110
Goudie, Andrew, 108
Greenberg, Barbara, 1–2

Harrison, Francis Burton, 7
Harrison Narcotics Act, 6–7, 41
Hart, Carl, 133
Helpern, Milton, 14
Heroin overdose, 11ff
  and the administration environment, 16–23
  perplexing features of, 13–16
Hodgson, Ray, 56
Homeostasis, 27
  and acute drug tolerance, 27–29
  and chronic drug tolerance, 29–30, 37–38

Jaffe, Jerome, 87–90
Jha, Prabhat, 127
Johanson, Chris-Ellyn, 99

K. J., case study, 12–13, 14, 16, 17, 21, 30, 38, 40

Index

Kesner, Raymond, 53
Kissin, Benjamin, 75
Kolb, Lawrence, 7–9, 22, 137

Laird, Melvin, 89
Langley, Leroy, 145
Leshner, Alan, 139
Lewis, Marc, 139

Macnish, Robert, 78–79, 81, 137
Mather, Increase, 3
McCusker, Christopher, 60–61
Mello, Nancy, 96–99, 100, 102, 104
Mendelson, Jack, 96–99, 100, 102, 104
Mike Fright, 70–71
Monforte, Joseph, 13, 14
Murphy, Morgan, 85

Narcotic Farm in Lexington, Kentucky, 8–9, 149n9
N. E., case study, 17–18
Newark, NJ, case study in, 19–20, 39
Nicotine and smoking, 1–2, 8, 37, 50–52, 66, 75, 106, 108, 119, 127–129
Nixon, Richard, 12, 84, 86–87, 89

O'Brien, Charles, 75, 114

Pavlov, Ivan, 30, 31–41, 43–47
Pavlovian conditioning. *See also* Conditional response
  acquisition of, 34–37
  and the "broken escalator" phenomenon, 68–70
  and drug overdose, 38–41
  in a "Little Rascals" movie, 70–71
Poulos, Constantine, 71–72

Recreational use of drugs, 132–133
Relocation of the addict and abstinence
  achieved by moving to a new residence, 81–84
  by addicted soldiers in the Vietnam War returning to civilian life, 84–91
  animal studies of, 92–93
Rieckmann, Traci, 55
Robins, Lee, 90–91
Rush, Benjamin, 3–4, 22, 68, 79
Russell, Michael, 128–129

Schasre, Robert, 82–83
Schuckit, Marc, 133–134
Schuster, Bob, 140–141
Schuster, Charles, 99
Shakespeare, William, 118–119
Smoking. *See* Nicotine and smoking
Solomon, Richard, 44–45
Steele, Robert, 85
Susceptibility to addiction, 133–136

Ternes, Joseph, 74
Tobeña, Adolf, 121
Twitmeyer, Edward B., 36

"War on drugs," 12, 84
Werner, Arnold, 15
Wikler, Abraham, 77–78
"Withdrawal symptoms" after detoxification, 73–78
"Withdrawal symptoms" as drug preparation symptoms, 71–73, 77, 113, 145

Yoked-control experiments, 105–106

Zador, Deborah, 40